SOCIAL MEDIA

STRATEGIES TO MASTERING YOUR BRAND –
FACEBOOK, INSTAGRAM, TWITTER, SNAPCHAT,

BY: DAVID KELLY

Free Bonus: Join Our Book Club and Receive Free Gifts Instantly

Free Bonus "Instant Access" Click Below For Your Bonus: https://goo.gl/UgTgnW

TABLE OF CONTENTS

INTRODUCTION

In 2006, Facebook expanded its already successful network of college students to include work networks. A year later, Twitter hit the scene as a new tool for businesses to interact with their customers. With the buyout of Instagram by Facebook in 2012, users of Instagram more than doubled and currently more than 300 million users are active on the app each month. Today, SnapChat is the new kid on the block with geofilters and stories to help businesses better connect with their audiences. In just ten years, social media has evolved drastically. Each day, more businesses are creating profiles and even more potential customers are as well. Social media is no longer a new concept for businesses but rather a necessity for building a reputation.

Online marketing has many advantages: the information travels fast, it is very cost effective, and there are no geographical boundaries; it is available for everyone. You've seen it time and time again. A new social media platform is released, and there's a mad dash to secure your business username and try to gain followers. Businesses then seek advice on growing their followers and converting potential customers after the fact. This is a social media fail! You need to be sure that you have a solid understanding of your brand. It takes more than a website in today's digital age. Social media is a tool for establishing your brand, not the other way around. Consumers are connected 24/7, and social media is how you can keep up. How many times have you heard a friend say they heard about a new product or found a cool article on a social media site? Always view social media as a golden opportunity to drive traffic back to your website and convert. Businesses can so easily create noise for consumers but with a solid social media brand, businesses can stand out and use social media to reach their goals.

Spend your time on social media platforms that best represent your brand. If you do not have an established brand, this guide will help you understand the importance of building a brand portfolio. Before venturing off into unchartered social media waters, understand what your business is and who you are trying to reach. Take the time to watch from a distance. Make observations of how other companies are using social media and engaging with customers. Develop an understanding of the demographics of each social network and what kinds of conversations are going on. Many businesses fail at social media due to a lack of planning and branding. Understand who you are and establishing yourself on social media will feel less daunting.

It's important to understand that you do not need to venture off onto every social media site. Read through examples of businesses that are using each social media site to promote their brand. Social media is not one size fits all. Use this guide as a resource for deciding which platforms will best help your company reach its goals.

There are particular social networking sites that are more suitable for showing your artistic skills, while others can introduce you to the software communities. Once you find the perfect site and the right group of people as your audience, you should strengthen this relationship in order to satisfy the customer in such a way that they become your marketers by spreading a good word about your brand, without you even paying them.

This guide will help you think critically about your brand and how to utilize social media to maximize your earning potential. We will focus on four of the top social networking sites – Facebook, Instagram, Twitter, and SnapChat. By the end of this guide, you will learn terminology related to each networking site and receive tips on planning, engaging and establishing a reputation on each. Equally important is being able to prove that the time and energy you are putting into social media is paying off. This guide will give you key metrics to measure your brand awareness and growth.

Social media brought us a new perspective on marketing and changed its course. Social media is a perfect platform for finding and/or establishing new brands. Since it is the age of Web 2.0, it is the time of selfbranding. Selfbranding tactics include creating and maintaining web pages, having both social and networking profiles, personal Web sites, and blogs. This also includes using search engine optimization techniques which would encourage access to and engagement with one's information. However, the social media designer should be aware of the cultural differences as well as the rules of the certain networks. The aforementioned, pages, profiles or forums of a certain brand should be updated on a regular basis in order to retain the credibility of the product. Today, anyone has the ability to contribute to marketing and branding, and in both positive and negative ways. After all, negative marketing is still marketing. This is possible because anyone has the opportunity to add content to others' profiles. This results in people not really having total control of their own page.

Managing the brand is a balance between protection, renewal, expansion and growth of the prototype, as well as creating new products and services. Essential for this is innovation, and it is crucial in order for the brand to endure.

On the other hand, the future of the brand and its values should be the main focus rather than developing technological competence and creating new products. Satisfaction of the customer should be first, and this can be a guideline not only when it comes to branding, but also in the design process. Social media can obviously be a tool for not only reaching the target audience but also for finding out more about the market and what customers really want. Besides, this can possibly help save the brand in the future.

The positive side is that social media is available around the world and free for everyone and is thus an ideal marketing channel for young artists and designers with a smaller amount of capital, or none at all. Reach the target group, gather the information you need, spread the word about your brand - your homemade cupcakes, your colorful necklaces, your beautifully painted portraits, your awesome photography skills - and there you are; the word is out. The information you shared once can be shared over again and become widely distributed. You may not even be aware of your own success. You need to find the proper channels for your brand and one of them may be more suitable then the other. Give them frequent attention, whenever you can manage, and make the customer a part of the development process and maintenance of your social media networks. The negative side is that bigger brands will still be found more often because they already have a large number of customers obtained from real advertising. But nothing is impossible.

Some of the designers may underestimate the power of the marketing channels that are free of charge, but these can do more good than harm. It is only necessary to use it right, to present a genuine idea, and to deliver it right. Then, let it grow in an organic way, to be spread like it is a first class rumor. That is what happened to the greatest social network we know today – Facebook - and tomorrow it may happen to your brand. Who knows?

Facebook's potential for profit was always there, from the moment its founder, Mark Zuckerberg, took it away from its North American college campus roots and made it available to others, meaning non-students could create profiles for themselves. Of course, Facebook has become more commercialized since that period, and it has given everyone the possibility to be heard. The original aim was to connect friends and make contacts, and step by step it included groups and fan pages for organizations, creating the world's largest closed network, which attracts advertisers from around the world every day. Soon, Facebook allowed users to write blogs, enticing more users to stay on the site rather than go to other blog hosting sites. This brought the feel of direct engagement and with this, companies could communicate directly with their customers and supporters, and it was a great way to bring together organizations and audiences.

The goals of social media branding

We all know that the primary goal of advertising a brand on social networks is to create a customer base. Customers use social networks; everything is about what you wear, what you have, what you eat, and where are you going, and this is seriously genius for all of you out there who are struggling to get the word out, to succeed in this crazy materialistic world. Yes, anything can be sold, because anything will be bought. However, social media allows anyone to post what they have to say. But this is survival of the fittest; Social Darwinism. Big and successful brands have the same possibility as some small homemade activity and it is not really a question of which one will be able to reach out more. Even with the same free profile page of your brand. So everything is in the hands of the customers. Any social media strategy must be in favor of the organization in two ways: internally and externally. There should be no 'us 'and 'them', so primarily, you need to build a sense of membership or citizenship within the organization and really feel like you belong there. You should encourage recognition, exchange of ideas and communication of brand values. Encourage the addressees to join in the dialogue and help you promote the brand. That dialogue can really help the organization discover and maintain a competitive benefit. You may want to include your vision of the brand within the bigger picture and create a differentiation for it. Check on whether the brand is being appropriately presented and understood by the customers. These costs create a path to building positive brand relations. Build the apparent quality of the brand, present your brand as strong and sustainable and build better awareness of the brand for the part of society that it has not yet reached.

As it was already said, it is the survival of the fittest, so, in theory, you should try to be genuine and unique, and present your brand in the same way, as it respectably deserves. You need to be heard. There are dozens of brands out there that managed in the market simply because they were heard of, not necessarily better. How many times have you seen a page on Facebook, for instance, that has around a million likes and sells the most beautiful accessories and clothes, and then it turns out to be a pretty good scam? Those pages that are just smoke and mirrors are soon uncovered, but still, many people get tricked. No refund! So you are left with a cheap, unflattering nightgown, which looks nothing like the elegant dress you saw in the picture. This is no different from the pre-election speech of any government candidate anywhere in the world. It only seems pleasant to the public ear, in this case, the eye. So don't be like them. People often check the blogs and social networks to look at and get a picture of the personalities behind the scenes. Actually, this may prove useful for the smaller organizations and companies since the main person of the company, for example, the owner or manager, can be the one who writes tweets and updates the Facebook fan page. With this in mind, an organization can be more open and responsive to audiences and consumer demands.

Everyone is going to look for something and someone they can trust. Maybe it is a recommendation from a friend they have confidence in, maybe it is the person behind the brand, maybe it is the way the brand employees are communicating with customers. You should observe everything and be aware of how you deliver your message to the audience. Don't leave unprofessional comments on your page, don't make preferences for one instead of the other, don't neglect your profile and certainly do not go into conflict discussions – you can only harm yourself.

Interestingly, there are brands that have no use for social media networks. For example, older people rarely use these networks, so brands geared towards an older population wouldn't really work as well here. Who knows, maybe this is genuine enough?

CHAPTER ONE

INTRODUCTION TO SOCIAL MEDIA BRANDING

Think about one of the world's most iconic brands, Starbucks.

Firstly, brands are led by a company's mission. Starbucks' mission is to inspire and nurture the human spirit; one person, one cup and one neighborhood at a time. Howard Schultz, CEO of Starbucks, believed the most powerful brands are built from the heart. Grounded by its mission, Starbucks' brand began to take form with a person, the consumer, in mind. From the coffee options available on the menu to the physical space of the café, Starbucks created an experience for its customers. Every Starbucks location uses particular plants, smells, sounds, colors and lighting. With social media growing, Starbucks took their brand to the digital sphere.

Each of Starbucks' social media platforms focuses on engagement. On Facebook, you can easily find your nearest location and scroll through selfies of consumers drinking Starbucks. Instagram is very similar with reposts of consumers' photos onto their main page. Starbucks responds to hundreds of tweets a day and has used consumer-created snaps in advertising.

If you were to do a search on Instagram for photos tagged #Starbucks, more than 19 million photos would pop up – none paid for by Starbucks. Engagement is one of the fundamental key indicators of success in social media branding. Starbucks made the consumer their brand, which makes it easy to stay consistent with their brand on social media. If you're still establishing your brand, then consider taking a similar approach to Starbucks and begin with the consumer in mind. On the other hand, if you already have an established brand, there are key elements to the Starbucks brand that you could borrow to communicate your brand better on social media. These elements will drive the content you post. Think critically about each item and consider how it relates to your business.

Since you probably don't have a team around you that takes care of marketing, especially a team for every appropriate social network for your business, try not to go all over the place and pick several networks that you will try hard to manage and to update, and then fail – either in advertising or production. And you don't need advertising if you have no product. So step by step, learn which outlets suit you and your business, choose a couple, and arrange your schedule so that it allows you to keep on top of them. But don't let it take too much of your time. try to link them and follow the steps below.

Consistency

The last thing you want to do is confuse your consumers. Eliminate confusion by using consistent messaging across all social media platforms that reiterate your brand. You want to use the same message over and over in order for it to be understood. Consumers receive a lot of messages, and they may only tune in sometimes. By staying consistent, you make sure that no matter when potential or existing customers are paying attention, they are receiving the same message.

Simplicity

Social media is making it easy for companies to overload consumers with content and messaging. Attention spans are shrinking and getting a consumer to pay attention to you is becoming increasingly difficult. Make it easier by keeping it simple. Narrow down your focus and keep your messaging succinct. Use plain language and short words. Get to the point and make a statement.

Visual appeal

Every social networking site is changing its display to become more visually appealing. Since the success of Pinterest, social networking sites have caught on to the actions of consumers. As consumers scroll through timelines, they are receiving hundreds of messages. Consumers will tune in and pay attention to strong, bold images. Determine what images are most in line with your brand and consistently promote those images to your audience.

Differentiation

Brand loyalty is the tendency of consumers to patronize the same brands. For consumers, although there are likely similar products and services, they continue to use the same brand, with no regard to convenience or price. This is because, in the mind of the consumer, there is something different about the brand they use in comparison to another. Make yourself stand out. With the example of Starbucks, their product is coffee but in the mind of the consumer, they aren't just buying coffee. They are buying an experience also.

Now that we understand that your brand must be consistent, simple, visually appealing and different, we can help you define your brand. Consider the following questions:

- What is your business?

- What are your business' core values?

- What is the delivery method of your product or service?

- Why would a customer care about your business?

As you answer these questions, keep your responses in line with the elements Starbucks showed us. Then lastly, ask yourself what emotion do you want your customers to feel when they think of your brand. Emotions can range from empowered to joy to hopeful.

Essentials to Build Your Brand on Social Media

Whatever your aim is, the people on social media first want to know who you are. You may take help of social media for selling products, persuading people to donate to a cause or gaining subscribers for the promotion of your brand, but the first question to be answered still remains the same- who are you in the first place? In fact, the answer to this question is always a major attraction to grab the attention of more and more people on social media and make them your followers.

Customers need someone to identify with the brand so let them know something about yourself. It could feel like a scam or fake if you were to leave out that part – don't be a ghost in your brand – you are the mastermind behind it. You are allowed to have some room for yourself.

However, any of the above mentioned actions need to first focus on the authority of your brand. So, how to ensure the authority of your brand which plays a pivotal role in ensuring your success on social media? And the best way to build your brand authority is possible through the optimum use of social media. As per the recent research done in the field of social media, more than 70% of brands have developed their immense trust in social media and plan to make huge investments in this field in the upcoming year. This move will certainly help such brands to build their good reputation in the market and reach new heights by making new followers.

So, are you ready to make a strong place in your industry and get good ranks on search engine giants like Google? Let's take a quick peek into the steps which you can follow to improve the strength as well as the popularity of your brand on social media:

1. Check if the Networks Chosen Support Your Brand Image.

As per the information provided by Convince and Convert, more than 22 percent of Americans make use of social media services multiple times a day, which specifies how a strong role is played by social media to build their brand. Yes, hundreds of networks are available nowadays, but you need to select the best as not every network can support your brand with similar efficiency. So, invest your time and energy only with on such networks which can really be fruitful for raising the popularity of your brand in the long run.

How to choose the best platforms for boosting your brand image? It is certainly one of the most essential steps as it plays a crucial role in supporting your brand image. Here are a few factors which must be taken into consideration before selecting a platform for supporting your brand image:

- **Facebook** – Until now, this platform has certainly proved itself to be the best platform for creating as well as promoting brand awareness. Undoubtedly, its wide usage all over the world gives one an easy way to make one's brand popular and reach millions in a go. Not only this, but Facebook also finds an upper hand over other networks for its heterogeneous user base. It gives you a wonderful opportunity to raise your brand's awareness among people of all the groups rather than being restricted to any particular segment. It automatically increases your brand's awareness and that too at a much faster rate.

- **Instagram** – It is a wonderful social networking site for such brands which basically rely on images for grabbing the attention of the customers. It is a great option for mainly retailers and clothing companies who depend on images for promoting their brands. It's great popularity among the youth who love to try a variety of clothes and mainly like watching images help a great deal in establishing one's retailing or clothing brands with the help of this social networking site.

- **Google+** - Though the popularity of Google+ didn't raise the temperature of social media platform as expected by many, it can certainly be a wonderful opportunity for such brands which are related to technology and want to strengthen their hold in the field. It is categorized in this way as over two-thirds of the people using this network are connected to the technology industry in some way or the other. So, if you have something to promote in the field of technology, it can certainly prove to be a reliable site.

- **Pinterest** - Is your brand related to jewelry or clothing? Then, Pinterest can definitely prove to be a good option for you. It is one of the favorites among women, and your clothing or jewelry brand can gain instant popularity on it.

- **Linkedin** - If you are a business oriented person and want to promote your company, no other platform can be better than Linkedin for you. It is also the first choice of people whose jobs demand promotion of business related content. It also provides a good platform for connecting with influential business groups which can help in strengthening the effectiveness of your brand.

- **GitHub** - If you have an interest in programming and computers, then you need to know that this is one of the greatest sites you will visit. Development of the GitHub platform began in October 2007. It is a social network for software engineers and enthusiasts. You can learn everything you need to know, present your work, share ideas with GitHub users who think alike, and you can do all that without unnecessary distractions.

- **Flickr** – This is a vast gallery for managing, organizing and presenting photos. You can either show your talents and skills in photography and hope you'll be noticed by some agency, or present your design on this high-quality photo sharing website. It is always worth a try.

- **Foursquare** – Foursquare is somewhat different, and works as an application rather than a website. It is a location service, a sort of check-in status, which allows you to have your customers notify their friends on social networks that they are at your business place – coffee shop, store, spa center or hairdressers salon. It has more than 25 million users. This means that you have to have a physical, real-life store location. Free marketing is fun.

- **AngelList** – This is a social network that helps startups find investors. It is a great way of presenting an idea for the job and to raise money for it. This page also allows browsing startup jobs. The only bad side is that it is only available in the United Kingdom, but hopefully, the expansion is coming.

- **Quibb** - This is a social network that connects job professionals by introducing them to various business topics, business news and up to date explanations. You can sign in with Twitter or a Google account. It includes members from almost

30,000 startups as well as companies such as Apple, Microsoft, Facebook, Google, LinkedIn, Amazon and Skype.

- **SnapChat** – This is an app which allows you to send photos or 10-second videos which disappear after some time. Brands are also using Snapchat to offer their customers an exclusive insider's peek at events or productions. Content is cheap to produce and is reaching a lot of viewers. Therefore, Snapchat offers brands a new opportunity to advertise and be in touch with their customers.

- **Tumblr** – This social network might not be your first choice for marketing purposes, but you might just be wrong, as it has been proven that Tumblr is a great blogging platform and social media tool all-in-one. Tumblr accounts are effortless in terms of personalization - it fits any brand's style and attitude, and it is easier to acquire followers than it is on other blogging sites.

2. Offer Interesting and Legible Content

Instead of giving boring details which very few may read, it is always recommended to give catchy details which are interesting to read and also easy to understand for others. Not everyone can understand your business terms so, keep it short and simple. In fact, the legibility factor will arouse the interest of the people, and they will feel curious to know more about your brand. Not only this, but such contents are also shared more giving wide popularity to one's brand. So, always remember to craft the content for social media in a highly precise and interesting manner which can quickly grab anyone's attention.

Now, let's discuss the points which should be taken care of while posting any kind of content on social media for the popularity of one's brand:

- Keep it precise and ensure that every single word of your content adds to the meaning of your brand giving it a powerful impression. In fact, each word should be talking in favor of your brand image. Yes, humor always plays an effective role in catching one's immediate attention so, it would play a magic wand in your brand popularity if you can use such content effectively in your brand promotion. However, if you are not sure about the overall effect of the humorous content or feel even a bit unsure about people's reaction, the idea must be pulled off immediately. It is better to avoid such humor filled content or images which can earn criticism of even one category of people as it may reflect your company in poor light. So, you need to be extra careful while choosing the content for the promotion of your brand as it is directly connected to the promotion of your business and reaching the masses.

- It's also an important to task to find out the type of content which can give you instant visibility on social networking sites. So, you need to spend some time in doing research to find out such content. It's been noticed that images click the minds of the visitors faster than blog posts, however; you need to check this by collecting relevant information on such areas before abiding by any particular promotion strategy for your brand.

- Always be ready to use visual content as it's a proven way to catch immediate attention. The latest researches in this field have also shown that articles and blog posts with attractive as well as informative images get almost 90% more views in comparison to those write ups which have only written content. The best example of this is one of the fastest growing social networking sites, Twitter which gets just double views on images as compared to texts posted on the site. The factor to be kept in mind is that it happens even when Twitter has seven times more text content than images posted on it. So, if you are thinking to promote your brand on social networking sites, the easiest and the most effective way will be to take an idea about the posts which have proved highly successful for certain brands. On the basis of that, you can site methods and modify those according to your requirements to ensure your success in the field. Such strategies not only help you in getting acquainted with tested and tried methods but also raise your confidence in the field.

For example, one of your competitors got a wonderful response on social networking sites by posting a blog titled "7 Quick Tips to Increase Website Traffic". So, instead of trying your hands on unproven titles, you can get a more effective blog post on the same subject and enrich it with better data to attract the attention of the customers towards your brand. Obviously, an intelligent customer will get attracted towards the better information which is enriched with data as well.

Now the question arises, how to find well performing content pieces related to your business? No need to worry as there are a number of tools to help you in resolving this issue. One of the most popular ones is BuzzSumo which helps in finding out the related successful content for your business on social media. In case you find difficulty in applying this technique, you can take help of the Backlinko blog's guide to getting a detailed idea about the subject.

3. Take Hold of Influencers

Posting highly catchy and attention grabbing content on your profile of the social networking site certainly plays a significant role, but it's just a part of the success strategy. In case your brand is not quite popular, all your efforts for its publicity may get lost somewhere. It's not that you won't be able to gather your own audience gradually with the help of good content posting, but it would certainly take a good deal of time.

Good news for you is that a much quicker approach to lure the influencers in your industry have already come into force. Some of the most popular ways used nowadays are:

- Specify the names of the influencers in your content pieces or cite their websites. It has proved to be a highly effective strategy to win the attention of the influencers with Google Alerts or other notifications. It notifies them about your content immediately after it's published.

- Tagging influencers referred by you in your content while posting on your social media profiles is also a wonderful way to catch attention and grow one's popularity.

- Emailing influencers after the publishing of your content to make them aware of their references used in your work is also proving itself as a great way for the promotion of one's brand as well as content.

So, what's the primary goal of all these actions? It's definitely to make your content piece popular among the users of various social networking sites. Yes, it will take a little time to build such relationships which can directly lead to influencer sharing, but if you keep on producing and publishing quality content, your efforts will soon start getting fruitful results.

4. Promote Content with Social Campaigns

Last but not the least, one can't deny the immense use of paid campaigns nowadays to gain instant popularity for one's brand. For this, you can take help of native advertising platforms easily available nowadays for growing awareness about your brand on social networking sites.

A large number of brands in their growing phase also use various other interesting strategies like contests to promote brand's visibility as well as generate leads.

For availing complete advantage of this strategy, you can also offer valuable incentives to your audience. It will not only help in encouraging user participation but also ensuring that the campaign launched by you gives due credit to all the participants.

Social media is undoubtedly one of the most effective ways of generating new leads. However, if you don't use it appropriately, there is a big chance of wasting your time and energy on it. It is the primary reason why following a strong social media strategy holds prime importance.

So, if you really wish to get fast and positive results in return for all your efforts made for brand building, you need to be consistent in sharing great quality content as well as leveraging the power of existing social media influencers. This will certainly give you great results in the long run.

Habitat for Humanity, a 501(c)3 nonprofit, has been awarded for their outstanding branding in the social services industry. Habitat's brand is positioned around their mission of bringing people together to build strength, stability and self-reliance through shelter. Although Habitat is a nonprofit, they are selling a product or service, in that they are in need of volunteers and financial donations. With each social media post, Habitat reinforces strength, stability, and self-reliance. Though those are feelings that their clients feel, they are pulling on the strength and stability that potential donors and volunteers may already have to move them to act.

One message Habitat uses is that "Every donation and helping hand is helping families create a place to call home." With the use of the word 'every', Habitat is staying consistent with their brand messaging and reinforcing people together. Habitat uses images of faces with houses in the background. Even when focusing on construction, which is reinforcing the "build" component of the brand, there is still a face because, in addition to building, Habitat brings people together. Due to its consistency, simplicity, visual appeal and differentiation, Habitat is successfully reaching its audience and converting.

In a business exchange, there are only three parties – the seller, the buyer, and the product. The act of completing a transaction – whether monetary or not – falls solely on the person who will buy. As humans, we make many decisions based on emotion. Therefore, your social media approach should focus on the buyer. Many businesses make the mistake of focusing on the seller or focusing on the product. Do not blast out information about yourself or what you're selling. Your role as a social media manager is to craft your message so that a potential buyer can see themselves at home using your product or service. Once you craft these great messages, you have to reach your target audience. Social media offers two options – organic and paid.

Organic posts are shared directly from a business page or profile. Followers see your post based on the algorithms of the site's newsfeed or timeline, which will vary from site to site. On the other hand, paid posts reach a specific audience with targeting criteria that you set. Each social network has its own paid post options with varying fee structures. The highest performing organic social media posts are short, visually appealing and relevant. We will discuss paid advertising on Facebook, Twitter, Instagram and Snapchat later in the guide.

Keeping the customer in mind, go to where they are online. The 80-20 rule encourages marketers to spend no more than 20 percent of your time on self-promotional activity and conversation and at least 80 percent on engagement that is not self-promotional. Look at relevant blogs and online forums. Make your active participants in these outside platforms part of your social media strategy. Write guest blog posts, make comments and answer questions. As you interact, make sure you have a way for people seeing you connect. Although you are following the rule of thumb and spending at least 80 percent on conversations that aren't promoting your business, by simply being visible, you have an opportunity.

You can easily and clearly direct customers to your social pages. Add links to your social channels on every page of your website. Do you blog on your business website? Add social sharing links to each post that are linked to your business username. Put your social media URLs in your email signature and on your business card. Any printed materials you use should have your social media links. Make it easy to be found. Social media reinforces your brand, so you want to have people connected with a portfolio that represents who your business is.

Social media is solely a tool for your brand strategy. You will give away more content than you receive but your efforts are part of a long-term strategy to have ongoing participation and increased understanding of your business and its brand. Your business goals may range from generating leads to converting social media followers into customers. Goals must be specific and measurable. Therefore, you want to be sure that as you move consumers from your social media to another platform, whether it be to your website to fill out a form, signing up for a newsletter or purchasing a product, that your potential customers are receiving consistent messaging.

Before moving to the next chapter, take the time to reflect on what we discussed on branding. Craft a message that tells the story of your organization in 140 characters. Your 'bio' or about us statement on social media may be the one opportunity you have to share your brand with potential or existing customers. Show the consumer who you are and what value you bring to them.

Below are some examples to help inspire you:

Berkshire Hathaway: Berkshire Hathaway Home Services is a real estate brokerage network built for a new era in residential real estate.

Krispy Kreme: To touch and enhance lives through the joy that is #KrispyKreme. The home of delicious doughnuts, coffee, and other treats.

Lulu: Empowering Indie Artists EST. 2002. Free Self - Publishing Digital Platform - Create • Publish • Share

MetLife: Helping customers around the world with insurance, annuities, and employee benefits.

Mr. Clean: With my line of products, I help people get rid of dirt faster and easier.

Raymond James: Raymond James is a financial services firm dedicated to one thing: Life Well Planned. We take pride in pragmatism and in our steadfast commitment to clients.

Walmart: Saving people money so they can live better. To buy products you've seen on this account, click the link.

Many take a keen interest in social media marketing campaigns to boost their business, but not all become successful. So, how to ensure your success with social media campaigns? Here are a few tips to achieve success with social media marketing:

- **Focus on Planning** – Planning plays a pivotal role in deciding your success on social media. For this, a proper keyword research should also be done using effective tools to ensure forwarding such ideas which will help in gaining the attention of your target audience.

- **Give Importance to Content** — Content is always the king when it comes to social media marketing. You must ensure that the information provided by you is liked by your customers and can arouse their curiosity in your products. Apart from using the text based content, you should give a lot of importance to create catching contents with photos and videos embedded. However, all the graphics used should be connected to the content.

- **Keep Your Brand Image Consistent** — With social media, you get a wonderful opportunity for marketing your brand image in a variety of social media platforms. Each platform has its unique way of dealing with marketing campaigns. However, you must not change the core identity of your brand image with every platform. The point here is to keep your brand image consistent to win the trust of the customers.

- **Use Blogging** — Blogging is a highly effective social media marketing tool which helps in sharing a wide range of informative content with readers. The best part is that even images can be used in the blogs to draw the maximum attention of the customers. It will be an amazing idea to convert your company blog into a social media marketing blog where you can share information related to latest social media efforts, events and contests.

- **Use Links** — The fact can't be denied that social media for marketing mainly depends on sharing of unique content to grab the attention of the followers. However, to catch more attention, you must do linking with outside articles as well. If you think that you are able to get valuable information from other sources which your target audience will find interesting as well as related to your business, you must go for it. Linking to outside sources also helps in improving trust and reliability. Not only this, but you also have a good chance of getting some links in return for it.

- **Identify Your Competitors** — Keeping an eye on the competitors helps in keeping you updated and following the latest tactics to attract customers. With this, you also get easy access to keyword research and industry related links which prove to be of great benefit in attracting the target audience. It also gives you social media marketing insight and an understanding of the social media marketing tactics used by your competitors. In case the tricks used by them are giving good benefits, you can also make it a part of your social media marketing.

- **Use Analytics to Measure Your Success** — It is not possible to measure your success in social media marketing campaigns without using any tracking data. For this, Google Analytics is a wonderful social media marketing tool which can help you in understanding how far you have been successful in using social media marketing tactics. In fact, it will also tell you the strategies which proved to be the most effective for you. You can also attach tracking tags to your social media marketing campaigns in order to monitor your success in an appropriate manner.

CHAPTER TWO

FACEBOOK

Of all the social networking sites for business, Facebook is one of the most complex. Facebook is constantly changing its algorithms which can make it difficult to reach your audience. This chapter will walk you through using Facebook for business from start to finish and provide tips on promoting your brand.

Facebooks offers profiles and business pages. Profiles allow you to add friends and are a two-way connection. On the other hand, Facebook users 'like' business pages and pages can then push content out to the people who 'like' them; however, pages are public, and anyone can follow a link to see everything that has been posted on the page. Business pages also allow you to set up paid advertising for Facebook and Instagram.

For one-man companies, such as realtors and media personalities, a profile may be enough. But for most, you will need to create a business page. Your business page needs to be linked to a personal profile. The advantage of using both your profile and page for business is that you can utilize your Friends list from your profile on your business page. With profiles, you can tag friends in business posts, invite them to events and to 'like' your page and also monitor conversations. Understanding your audience based on the content they post is not available with business pages.

Grow your network by first connecting with professional contacts on your personal profile. Add media contacts, collaborators, potential clients and other people in your industry. You can also find friends in Facebook groups or in the comments of other Facebook Pages.

It is understandable to want to keep your personal and professional Facebook lives separate. You can create Friend lists and control what different lists see. To create a friend list, go to *Account > Edit Friends*. You canhave as few as one list for professional contacts, or make 100 lists and segment in different ways. When posting, you can exclude lists from seeing a post or target and make sure that one list does see your post. After you create lists, they will appear in the left-hand toolbar. When you click on a list, you have a dedicated newsfeed from the friends on that particular list.

You do not need to wait until you have the perfect personal profile to create a business page; however, you will need to have an account in order to create a Facebook business page. Admins are people who can post on behalf of the business page and make design changes. Since your personal profile is linked, you automatically become the admin, but you can add additional admins.

Step-by-step, we will explore creating your Facebook page and discuss opportunities along the way for branding your page.

When you first go to create a page, you can set your page up for a local business, company or organization, artist or entertainment. The main difference between local business is that you are searchable by location, as opposed to the company, which is searchable by category. If you have a physical location that you use for conducting business, then create a local business page. If your product or service is available anywhere, create a company page.

Next, there are four steps to complete the initial set-up:

1. About: There is no character limit on Facebook's About section. Use the bio you created at the end of chapter one to guide this section. Stay true to your brand by sharing your goal and using consistent language. From the examples in the last chapter, Raymond James expanded on their 140-character description and wrote:

Our business is people and their financial well-being. In pursuit of their goals, we offer the independence to serve them objectively, the integrity to serve them well, the conservatism to serve them responsibly and the commitment to put them first.

2. Profile Picture: Choose a photo that represents your brand. Most companies use their logo as a profile picture, but you can also have a picture of your product. The ideal size for a Facebook profile picture is 180 pixels x 180 pixels.

3. Add to Favorites: Makes access to your page easier.

4. Preferred Page Audience: Part of completing your brand strategy is making sure you reach an audience that is most likely to connect with your brand. Your target audience is comprised of your ideal customer based on demographics like age, gender, occupation, hobbies, geographic location, race and marital status. Based on work that you've already done; you may have an understanding of your current audience. Be sure to target this group but also target groups that may not currently connect with you that you feel social media will help. For example, if you're selling running shoes but mainly 40-year-old mothers are buying your shoes, and you believe men would also like your shoes, include men in your target

audience. Facebook's preferred page audience allows you to select locations, age, gender, interests, and languages.

Next up is the fun part, the design.

1. Make sure your profile is 100% complete. Facebook encourages businesses to add contact information and descriptions of the business (beyond the About statement).

2. Add a Call-to-Action. On the cover photo, you have the option to add a button. There are various call-to-actions you can add to your page: Book Now, Contact Us, Send Message, Shop Now, Sign Up and Learn More.

3. Create a Cover Photo. Facebook's cover photo is an engaging image you use as a header on your page. The ideal size is 851 pixels x 315 pixels. What image best represents your brand? If you want consumers to feel reassured, perhaps you use an image from a client meeting. If you want customers to feel excited, consider your product with an intriguing backdrop. If you're still working on building your photo library, you can find stock photos on websites like Creative Commons and

iStockPhoto. Canva, which is an image creation site, also offers options for creating visually appealing graphics.

Lastly, plan your content and engagement strategies. Your Facebook updates should include a mix of text, photos, videos, and links. Using an RSS feed, you can curate content from like-minded businesses and share relevant content to your audience. By tagging the source in your post, you can catch their attention. Cross-promotion is a useful tool when you're growing your audience and raising brand awareness. As you share content from others, they may begin to look to you for content to share as well. Therefore, it's important to have original content that relates to your brand and is shareable.

Shares are just one way that consumers can engage with your brand. Facebook users can also like and comment on your posts. When users are commenting on your posts, you are making serious traction in your efforts to master your brand on social media. Comments are a conversation. As opposed to a megaphone approach, which many companies often take and simply push out content rather than receiving feedback, a conversation is a two-way interaction. Please remember that your consumers are human, and it is our nature to want to interact. You will see the most growth when you engage and incite emotion. Once you've mastered content and engagement, focus on the conversation.

The average organic Facebook post is seen by only 16 percent of the page's followers on average. To defy this statistic, you want to make sure the right audience is connected with you on Facebook. Do not blast out to your family that lives miles away. Maximize your reach by getting your most loyal customers and most promising leads to like your page. Once they've connected, develop a social media strategy that provides value for them. Your social media strategy will determine what content your audience most wants to see when are the best times to post and who are key stakeholders that you can tag. Tagging is great for organic growth because it puts your message in front of the friends of the user you tag.

If you have funds available, you can pay to promote social media posts or create Facebook advertisements. For businesses, the best approach is to look at which of your posts perform the best organically and "boost" those posts. High organic reach means you already have interesting and engaging content. If your current customer base has already connected, then your chances of connecting with new consumers who want your product or service are higher.

Facebook offers four types of paid posts: Marketplace Ads, Page Post Ads, Sponsored Stories and Promoted Posts. Marketplace advertisements are found in the right-hand sidebar as you scroll through your timeline. Page post advertisements appear on users' newsfeeds. These posts blend in with your newsfeed and look as though they may be regular status posts from a brand you follow. Sponsored stories reach you if a friend has engaged with a company. Engagement could like the page, liking a post, sharing a post or commenting. Lastly, promoted posts, or "boosted posts" promoted existing Facebook posts to a larger audience.

When creating your advertisement, define your call-to-action. Are you generating leads? Then you want consumers to sign-up. Are you selling a product? Then you want consumers to shop now. Do you have a cool product story to tell and want people to see it on your website? Then you want consumers to learn more. Beyond deciding on the call-to-action, decide who you want to respond. This will determine your target audience for your advertisement.

Next, select a visually appealing image. Your image cannot contain more than 10% text. Facebook reviews each advertisement and your artwork will be denied if it contains more than the allowed text amount. Use compelling copy to go with your image. Ask a question or make a bold statement but make sure that your messaging is consistent. Lastly, select how long you want the add to run for. You can pay-per-click (CPC) or pay-per-impression (CPM). CPC is a model where you'll pay each time someone clicks on your ad, as opposed to CPM where you pay based on the number of times your ad is shown.

Whether paid or organic, having strong Facebook posts will increase your visibility in the market. Using Facebook to raise brand awareness couples traditional marketing techniques of content curation and sharing with modern techniques of engagement. If consumers are landing on your Facebook page, you want them to understand who you are and want to connect with you. The brand you put before them is what they're signing up for. Once you've gotten them to like your page, your content must continue to reinforce who you are and what you do.

Be sure to ask that your customers add your page to their favorites. It is a simple click, and this way they are not going to miss your posts in their news feed. Try to post something every day. If you cannot manage to be online all the time, which is probably the case, schedule your posts when you have enough time, upload pictures, videos or statuses and set the time and date of their publishing. Scheduled posts can be shared between 10 minutes and 6 months from the time you create them, depending on when you schedule them. Set up an automatic message for your customers who are trying to reach you. Instead of making them wait for your response, let them know you are away and that you will contact them soon. This will make them feel comfortable in asking more questions about your brand and will avoid them feeling neglected. Plus, it will seem more professional.

How to Use Facebook to Grow your Business

Nowadays, it sounds irrelevant to ask if the person has a Facebook profile or not as almost everyone has it. Yes, so you have a Facebook page, but are you using it to its fullest? Are you even aware that it can be effectively used to grow your business with a lot less effort than you have been putting until now? So, beside posting updates, there are numerous ways in which you can use your Facebook page for creating awareness among people about your business brand and gain popularity for it.

Let's have a quick look at some of the most effective ways in which a Facebook page can be efficiently used for growing one's brand or business:

- **Ask for Testimonials and Reviews and Post on Website**

It helps a great deal in improving your brand name and grabbing the attention of the customers to know more about it. If you have used your Facebook page for promoting a local business, you also get a wonderful option embedded in the page to collect testimonials and reviews from your customers. Though it may be difficult to motivate customers to review your business page for earning some incentives, however, a sign can be put at your business place to make customers aware of the option of review your business on your Facebook profile page.

The list of benefits doesn't end here. Apart from having a Facebook page filled with reviews of the customers, some of the selected best reviews can also be posted on your website to roll the eyeballs of the visitors as almost everyone gets interested to know the review of a website to judge the value and performance of its products.

Let's also understand how to add a review to your website yourself. First of all, you need to click on the timestamp of the review and then click the drop-down arrow at the top right. After that, you are required to select the Embed Post option. To make the process simple, it is important to specify here that the Embed Post option may be hidden under the More Options link in the drop down menu which must be checked to find the right option.

In the last step, the Embed Post code can be used to add your best Facebook reviews to your website's testimonials page. It will help to a great extent in upgrading the value of your business as well as increasing its popularity.

- **Strike Connection with Your Audience**

So, what's the most essential element for using your Facebook page for business? It's to connect with your audience first. Now, the audience on your page consists of a good variety as it includes the fans of your business, fans of your content, current customers, former customers as well as potential customers. The post created by you or posted on the site should keep in consideration all these people as the first priority is always to connect with the audience.

If we follow the traditional method of audience engagement, the rule followed is always 80/20 which means that eighty percent of the content is created keeping in perspective the audience and the remaining 20% is for the promotion of the business. The lesser part can also be used for marketing, sales or self-promotion purposes.

The above explanation clearly states how important it is to engage with your audience for the promotion of your business page. To grab the attention of the audience, you can motivate their participation by posting catchy and informative content related to your business consistently.

To win a loyal and engaged audience for your posts, you must create posts relevant to your niche. It will also ensure to win the attention of your audience in that 20 % of posts which are basically used for the promotion and creating brand awareness about one's products and services.

You should also make sure that you actually interact with your audience by replying to their comments and giving them the type of content they want. Keep track of the comment box on your posts to find out what your audience likes or doesn't like about your posts and feed them the type of content they seem to like best.

If one of your posts gets an extraordinary number of likes and shares, try to find out why that is. This will help you make similar posts in the future and gain even more exposure by regularly posting the type of posts that your customers seem to respond well to and by avoiding those they seem to hate.

Keep in mind however that there is no such thing as bad publicity. Is there a persona in your industry that people seem to genuinely hate? Perhaps posting about them may actually give you positive results as the audience will jump in with negative comments, which will again give your posts exposure, and that's exactly what you want.

- **Use News Feed Ad Placement for Maximum Benefit**

Facebook offers an option to place ads within the news feed in the right column. The only requirement for this is your link must be added to a **Facebook page** to display it in the news feed. In case you don't have a Facebook page, you can only take the benefit of ad placement service in the right column.

In news feed ads, your page is used as the source of the ad by the Facebook. It will give your target ad audience an option to like your page apart from connecting with the main objective of your advertisement.

- **Take Audience Feedback**

It's always better to get an overview of the customer's expectations and giving the best to fulfill their demands. So, how to get an accurate feedback of the potential or current customers about one's brand or product? The best way is to survey them on Facebook. The survey method not only gives a path to the customers to connect with your page but also helps you in understanding the expectations of your customers in a better way.

To take the poll of your audience, it is always better to make a standard post on the page for the same and it must be for free. If you find it time taking, then you can also opt for Facebook polling apps which are simple to use and even the audience can understand it easily. Between these options, choosing anyone depends on your choice of compiling the answers on your own or getting readymade answers through the app. Also, for collecting personal information like email IDs, you need to ensure that it's not done publicly on the page, and all the privacy concerns are adequately followed in it.

- **Utilize Your Facebook Page for Blog Comments**

It becomes a difficult and tiring job handling spam on one's business blog as most of the comments are for the sake of promotion and divert the attention of the audience. To tackle such problems, the Facebook page can be one of the best options for receiving blog comments. To simplify the process for the audience, a link can be added telling about the post on Facebook at the end of every blog post.

It's necessary to ensure that the link points to a post published on your Facebook page wall about that post. The best part is that it allows turning off the comments option on your blog when it's not required. Not only this, but it also helps in building a strong fan base and bringing organic engagement on your blog through really interested readers. It has an additional benefit as well. People who will notice the tailing discussion on your Facebook page around a particular post, they would feel curious and definitely click once to read the content of the blog post.

- **Use Facebook Page to Comment on Others' Business**

If we talk about the blog comments, more than 128,000 websites consider Facebook as a better platform than standard comment platforms like Wordpress which are equipped with built in content management systems.

Whenever you comment on a blog that's related to your business, it will always be in your interest to use your Facebook page for commenting rather than your personal profile. So, how to do it? It only requires you to select your page from the drop down menu given next to the Comment button and post your comment there.

So, what's the benefit of doing this? Using your Facebook page gives an immediate invitation to the people who like your comment to like your business page as well which is not possible when you connect with your personal profile. If you have any admin for your business page, he or she can also use your page for commenting on blogs using Facebook comment option.

Actually, when you post comments using your personal profile, your business page gets automatically linked next to your name. In fact, your position becomes also visible to others if you've given information about your current employer in the Work and Education section.

Not only this, but you can also tag other Facebook pages within your comment. For complete safety from any kind of spam while using this feature, you are free to use it only when applicable to your needs.

- **Use Facebook Page to Curb Negative Results on Search Engines**

Are you facing negative results in searches for your name on search engines and it's giving a bad name to your business? Your Facebook can be a sigh of relief for you. As Facebook is a strong domain, you can use a page with your business name to improve your rankings in the search results.

It may be possible that your Facebook page doesn't rank immediately after your website, but it will definitely fall within the first ten search results. So, it will reduce at least one negative result about your business name from the first page of search results.

So, there are innumerable ways to use your Facebook page for driving benefits in an easy manner. In case you haven't yet made your Facebook page, create one today and start using it in the number of additional beneficial ways explained above.

CHAPTER THREE

TWITTER

If you want to know what's happening in the world at any given moment, Twitter is the place to go. With only 140 characters to deliver your message, users share news and opinions and interact with others instantly. As a business, you can quickly reach new and existing customers. People may already be sounding off on your product or service. Twitter makes it easy for you to find these people and either respond to comments or introduce them to your company. We will take a look at the basic functions of Twitter and later discuss how your business can best utilize the app to fit your brand.

Twitter has five main functions: your timeline, notifications, moments, messages and your profile. The basis of Twitter is 140-character 'tweets' that are messages that may contain text, photos, links, and videos. Tweets are sent out by users. Every user has a 'handle', which is your username on the site. Other users can 'tag' you in posts by putting an '@' symbol before your handle. This is called a mention. Users make the choice to follow other users. As a result, every tweet you send and the accounts you follow send populated information to your timeline. Twitter will make recommendations for people to follow but you can also use your email list to find followers. A good tip is to load any email addresses you have into a contact list on your email provider and link to Twitter to find those accounts. Once users see you are on Twitter, they may immediately follow back. If you see slow growth from this method, consider sending a tweet to active accounts and let them know you're on Twitter and what they'll gain from following you.

Your timeline is in chronological order from newest to oldest. Every tweet by another user has the option for you to retweet, quote a tweet and like. Retweets share a tweet from someone else to your followers. Quoting a tweet allows you to add your own comment to the tweet. A like is an acknowledgment of a tweet. Liked tweets are bookmarked, and you can easily find them again. If someone mentions you using the '@' symbol, then those tweets populate in your notifications. You will also receive a notification if anyone follows you, and retweets or likes your tweet.

Many tweets contain a hashtag. Using the '#' symbol, user's hashtag conversations. Many brands will use a hashtag to promote a campaign or to reinforce an ongoing message. For example, Coca-Cola's "Share a Coke and a Song" campaign encourages consumers to share photos of them drinking coke with friends. The bottles have song lyrics, so consumers have creatively shared videos of them singing the song lyrics. Photos and videos are grouped together using the hashtag #ShareaCoke. This campaign began with personalized bottles of Coke and sent consumers on a chase to find a bottle with their name on it. Selfies with their personalized Coke bottles were very popular. Coca-Cola's brand inspires happiness, and this is reiterated through light-hearted social campaigns.

When you search a hashtag, all of the tweets that are tagged will show, with the exception of tweets made by private accounts. When many people use a hashtag simultaneously, it becomes a trending topic. You can change your settings to see the top ten trending topics by region, state or country. By joining in on trending topics, you increase your visibility. Trending topics no longer need a hashtag. If you join in the conversation about something that others are talking about, for example, a Golden State Warriors game, and you used the phrase 'Golden State Warrior' or 'GSW', while others are doing the same, then it is likely to become a trending topic.

Tweet chats use hashtags and are an opportunity for organic advertising. Usually focused around a general topic, tweet chats are a live conversation between like-minded Twitter users. The conversation is moderated by a host that sets the date and time. Join in on conversations that are relevant to your business. There are tweet chats available for different industries. As you share your insights and opinions, be sure that you are representing your brand. A Google search will tell you what Tweet chats are coming up in your industry and who's hosting. If you do not see any active companies hosting Tweet chats, take a look at the hashtag to see what conversations were had and who attendees were. Tweet chats are an opportunity to raise awareness, connect with potential customers and overall expand your social media reach.

There are five main post types: photos, quotes, status updates, videos, and links. One social media strategy is the rule of 4-1. Select one main post type that your followers can expect to see from you. Every fourth post, switch it up and post using a different type. This strategy keeps you consistent, while also providing enough varied content that your followers will not get bored.

The beauty of Twitter is that new content appears every second. However, this may pose a challenge to marketers. As you work on maximizing your brand on Twitter, remember that social media marketing is not a 9-5 job. Social media updates constantly and when your consumers are online being when you should be online. There are many social media publishing apps available that help you schedule tweets in advance, such as Tweetdeck, Hootsuite, SproutSocial, and Buffer. Social media publishing apps are great for staying organized and ensuring you have frequent messages that reinforce your brand, but you must also monitor your brand on Twitter.

Social media monitoring is of true importance on Twitter. Messages are exchanged so frequently that it is likely that you may miss something. Whenever possible, respond quickly to mentions, thank new followers and share content that is relevant to you or uses a hashtag you actively promote. The more you engage, the more you raise awareness of who you are. Another tip is to utilize Twitter's search function. Users may not know your Twitter handle, but they still talk about you on the network. You can search for your company name. If there are multiple companies with your name, you can narrow the search down by looking for who's talking in your area. Also, search for common misspellings of your company name and products. Mistakes are a perfect opportunity to educate and raise awareness.

Another tool offered by Twitter is Twitter lists. Twitter lists allow you to monitor different categories. Similar to an RSS feed, you can populate content from similar accounts to help with monitoring. Lists can be public or private. Examples of Twitter lists include media lists, national news personalities, and sites, industry news and competitors. Lists help you organize your audience and also easily join in conversations that are relevant to your brand.

Like all social media networks today, Twitter offers paid advertising opportunities. If you're going to spend money on social media, spend it on advertisements and not followers. It's better to pay for your ad to reach 100 real, engaged followers, then to blast out an organic tweet to 30,000 random followers. Remember, your goal is to convert.

Twitter ads are available for any account. Advertisements look like any tweet you would see on your timeline, but it is marked as "sponsored." This means that even if you're not following a brand, you see the post because it is sponsored. You design your ad campaign based on your goal. Objectives to select from include followers, website clicks and conversions, tweet engagements, app installs, leads on twitter and promoted tweets. After you select your goal, you can compose a new tweet or select an existing tweet. Additionally, you can create a Twitter Card. If you have a call-to-action, you will design your Twitter card with an image, call-to-action button, and link headline. Twitter Cards are paired with your paid tweet.

Next step is setting up your audience targeting. Similar to Facebook, you can drill down on the demographics you want to reach with your paid tweet. You can micro-target with specifics like accounts using a specific keyword or followers of another Twitter account. Lastly, you set your time frame and budget, then launch!

Twitter advertising is exciting because it's still relatively new. Additionally, Twitter's main activity is done from a mobile device. As a result, it is very easy to generate leads because when a user signs up, they are signed up using the email address registered to the account.

Although you only have 140 characters per tweet to connect with audiences, using the brand elements discussed in chapter one, you can still make real progress towards raising awareness for your brand. Even the biggest company fails trend for two days and then disappear. New content is constantly generated on Twitter. If you can keep up, consider maximizing Twitter to meet your goals.

Quick Proven Tips to Boost Your Brand or Business with Twitter

It's quite possible that you may have been using twitter for quite some time for marketing your brand or business, but didn't find see much growth in your business or could make a good profit. It may also be possible that you have been trying to use it for the sake of promotion but in vain.

So, where does the problem lie? Yes, it lies in your way of using the site. It shows that you are not well versed with strategies which can be used to grow or promote one's brand on this site. Instead of spending time in researching the proven methods, here is a list of some tips which can be easily used by anyone:

1. Careful Selection of Hashtags

Yes, you heard it right! Hashtags are not a matter of bygone days, but hold primary importance even today if you are using Twitter.

As before, the usage of hashtags on Twitter should be kept limited, and it needs to be very careful chosen. While picking hashtags, you must ensure if it's relevant to your tweet. The best way to make optimum usage of hashtags is to use only when a given hashtag is already trending.

If you need help in choosing appropriate hashtags that can help in the promotion of your business, the websites like Ritetag and Hashtagify can prove to be of immense. It helps in searching the best related hashtags which can be used in one's tweets.

2. Understand and Analyze the Most Appropriate Time to Tweet

Like the trick you follow on Instagram, you should also be aware of the best time to tweet when using Twitter. Just like when posting on Instagram you check the best time, you need to know the most appropriate time to tweet as well in order to ensure that your tweets get actually read by the target audience.

How to choose the best time? You can judge this by having a clear idea about the time zones where your perspective customers are located. There is a wonderful tool called Twitter analytics available for twitter users which can help in giving a proper analysis of time zones of your current followers. Based on their time zones, you can get an idea when most of your followers will be online. Apart from this, Tweriod is another tool which can be used to check the number of times your audience comes online.

3. Make Optimum Usage of Twitter list function.

Twitter list is a wonderful tool for grouping accounts together which belong to a particular niche, which makes it easier to find relevant content to retweet. The best part about this app is that it also gives the option to subscribe to someone else's list apart from creating one's own Twitter list.

4. Add value in your retweets

It's okay to retweet if you give credit to the original post. However, it becomes important to make it valuable as well which can be done not by simply retweeting a quote, but by including a reaction or opinion as well. It can also be used as an amazing opportunity to connect with your brand.

5. Tweet testimonials.

Testimonials always play a powerful role in promoting one's business or product. Posting words right from the mouth of the customers and fans always double the chance of catching immediate attention of expected followers and buyers on Twitter. Such acts are always helpful in enhancing one's credibility and winning the trust of the people around.

6. Set a Limit on Link Usage

As people have got too much used to use links even when not required for marketing their products, you must set a limitation to yours to suffer similar kind of ignorance from others. As it's said too much usage of anything annoy others and even make them ignore you so, consider this statement seriously. The best way is to use links only when it can add value to your post. It will, in fact, double your chance of getting more clicks.

7. Consistent Interaction with Local Influencers.

Your local news media offers a wonderful opportunity to get your post retweeted. You can't ignore the importance of the local reporters and journalists who can play a pivotal role in boosting your brand impression.

8. A Good Profile Photo and Branding Your Twitter Page can do Wonders

Want to boost your credibility? Using an amazing profile picture, attractive company logo and a branded Twitter page can win hearts of many. In a world where everyone is doubtful about originality, these things will help in winning the trust of others.

After going through these simple tips, you can't deny the fact that using Twitter for the promotion of your brand or your business can be tremendously useful as well as fun.

9. Interact With Your Audience

You want your audience to interact with your Twitter profile so why not interact back? If you have dedicated followers who are commonly retweeting and commenting on your tweets, do your best to make them feel special. In fact, if you have the manpower, make every customer who engages with your tweets feel special by replying to their comments and helping them out with any issues.

In the long run, it will probably cost you very little to interact with your customers, and it will create an image of you as someone who truly cares about their users, which in turn is likely to lead to even more users interacting with you, leading to more exposure and completely free marketing.

10. Create Competitions and Promotions

Companies have been giving away free products and services to their customers for many decades, but social media gives you new opportunities to get massive exposure for very little money by using competitions and promotions online.

You can easily throw twitter competitions that give away your product, free money, vouchers or bonuses in return for retweets, comments or any other kind of innovative interaction you can think of. The more followers you have, the more likely your competition is to drag hundreds of new followers in to follow you.

Make sure you ask every follower who wants to take part in the competition to retweet your competition so that others can see it and follow you in order to take part. Once the competition is over, you can get the winners to retweet and comment to get even more exposure and just a few free products may give you hundreds of new followers, which is an excellent value to any company.

CHAPTER FOUR

INSTAGRAM

Instagram is one huge photo album with content from users all over the world. You can find photos and videos of anything. Posts with common themes are tied together using hashtags. The chances are that there are already users posting pictures and videos that connect to your products and services. After you've mastered the basics of branding, you can delve deeper into using the unique qualities of Instagram to better reach your audience.

Instagram is unique, in that you can only post to your profile page using a mobile device. Users can find you using a browser by visiting Instagram.com/your username. As a user, you can like and comment from a browser. There are five main screens in your Instagram app. From left to right, there's the home screen, discover page, camera, activity and your profile. The home screen is where you can view your friends' photos and videos. With a timeline display, you scroll up and down to view what has been posted. Instagram has played with different algorithms but currently, you view photos and videos in chronological order from most recent to oldest. Your discover page is how you search for and add friends. Based on photos you and your friends like, Instagram will make suggestions on posts you may like also. The discover page is an opportunity to connect with potential customers and influencers.

Camera is where you add content to your profile. You can upload from your phone or snap a photo or video straight into the app. After you've selected a photo or video, you can add a filter. Filters give an intensified, photographic look to images and videos. There are more than a dozen options to choose from. After deciding if you'd like to add a filter, you can add a caption and tag other users. You can tag people in your caption using '@' or using "Tag People." If you are using the "tag people" function, your photo will be added to the profile of the user you're tagging under "Photos of Me."

Next, the activity feed has two screens – Following and You. The Following section shows the recent activity of your friends. You can see what pictures and videos people you follow have liked, as well as new users they follow. The You section shows your activity. You can see who likes your photos and videos, who has followed you (or requested to follow you), comments or tags you in a photo.

Your Instagram profile is a collection of every photo and video you've ever posted. It can be found on the last screen of the app. This screen is where you can edit your profile and profile settings, including your bio and link. A bio reinforces your brand. Your bio is where you can briefly share information about your company. You can also add a link to your profile. The link could be your website or a landing page. If you are planning to post about a new product or service and want to direct your Instagram followers directly to that link, it is best to change out your link. Unfortunately, you cannot add links to the captions of your photos.

Instagram has two privacy settings – private and public. For your business, you want to make sure that you have a public profile. Private accounts do not allow people who aren't following them to see their content. Users can see your bio and username, but they can request access. The advantage to a private account is that you can more easily monitor who is following your brand; however, the use of other features like hashtags and photo mapping is limited. As you grow your brand, you want to make yourself easily accessible, so opt for a public profile.

As you begin to grow your Instagram audience, be sure you have recent photos and are consistent with how often you are posting. You want interesting, relevant and eye-catching content. Users connect with faces, but if your brand doesn't fully capture the face of anyone, then the best photos are high-quality with bright lighting. Blurry and dimly-lit photos are quickly passed over. Your goal with Instagram is to engage your audience enough that they receive some takeaway, whether it's a hashtag you're using or to follow the link in your bio.

Follow accounts that are similar to yours and engage with these accounts. Like and comment on photos. Look at who is following similar accounts and follow them first. A fraction of the people you follow will follow you back if they can see the relevance of your profile to them. This is why it's important to make sure you have recent and frequent content as you're growing your followers.

Paid advertising on Instagram is set up and managed through Facebook. In order to set up your ad, you must have a Facebook page linked to your Instagram account. You can link by visiting your Facebook business page and clicking *Settings*. Then login to your Ads Manager account. Ads Manager is available through Facebook. Under Ads Manager, click *Power Editor*. You will need to download Power Editor in order to create your ad. After figuring out the technical aspects of creating your ad, you will follow the same process you use for creating Facebook ads. You can even create Facebook and Instagram ads simultaneously. This cuts down on time for setting your audience and creating a copy. The only change would be the size of the image for your advertisement.

As opposed to the other social media platforms described in this guide, Instagram is completely comprised of the visual appeal element. Exploring the use of Instagram to grow your brand will force you to think about the visual component to your brand. Many businesses overlook this part and rely on stock photos to tell their visual story. While that may work when you're first starting out, as you define your brand, it may deter you from your goals. If your brand is built on authenticity, consider allocating dollars for a few professional photoshoots that capture the true essence of your brand. Photos that are unique to you and your company will only reinforce what your brand is to your target audience.

Tips to Master your Brand with Instagram

To promote your brand and business, Instagram may be a recent addition to social media sites, but it has already become a favorite of many. Whether it's from an interesting interaction point of view or promoting one's brand in a simpler way, the efficiency it shows in both has been grabbing everyone's attention. If you are making use of social media to reach your customers, Instagram can't be ignored at all.

The recent searches find Instagram to be 15 times more efficient in attracting customers and marketing one's business as compared to Facebook, Twitter and Google+. It's unbelievable to see its tremendous growth in such a short span of time, but it's definitely true. You can't ignore the fact that a simple photo sharing application has emerged as one of the key sales channels at present.

Let's discus a few tips to grow your brand and business with the help of Instagram:

1. Make a Large Community Base

To everyone's amazement, only thirteen percent of Internet users have Instagram accounts at present, but more than 75% of the world's topmost 100 brands are already on Instagram. This figure shows that your current and potential customers may also be available on this site.

Here are a few ways by which you can promote your brand or business on Instagram:

2. Use Audience-Targeted Hashtags

Hashtags are a wonderful way to showcase one's ideas, concepts or conversations in a group. It's also an easy way to look for people who post on topics you may be interested in.

By using suitable hashtags in your updates, you can find an easy way to reach people showing keenness in your products. The best way to ensure maximum benefit is to use hashtags that not only give the details of your photos and business but are also famous on Instagram and are actively searched for by people.

Now, the question arises, how to find the most appropriate hashtags for promoting one's business? For this, you can opt for a free online service like Iconosquare or Websta which provide a list of relevant hashtags based on one's needs.

You can make efficient usage of such lists to find the best 10-20 hashtags related to your brand, business or product. And this way, you can get the most suitable hashtags for promoting your business.

3.   Ensure Application of Right Filters

The biggest problem is that people are not even aware of the way how Instagram filters may affect the engagement of the audience. Generally, people post what they find attractive and most of the times such posts turn out to be filters which affect the overall interaction on the site.

As per a recent study published by TrackMaven, a number of photos found with the Mayfair filter or the Inkwell filter received more likes and comments.

It is true that for different businesses, the target audience also differs. So, it is highly recommended to experiment with various filters and use an Instagram management tool to check the filter which can prove to be the most popular for your business needs.

4. Post at Climax Times

It is not only with Instagram but with all the social networking sites. For this, you need to be aware when your target community will mostly be online and on Instagram. It helps you in judging the best time to post and acting accordingly. One of the best websites which is immensely useful in choosing the peak times for increasing engagement is IconoSquare which gives an optimization report based on one's engagement and posting history in the past.

You get a detailed report in which black circles represent the times you're posting, and light-gray circles represent the level of engagement those posts received in the past. The best times or the peak times to post are shown by the biggest light-gray circles which are calculated based on your followers' engagement on the site.

5. Interact With Competitors' Followers

So, the catch is to interact with those who are following your competitor's Instagram account. Why is it required to be done? The main reason is to convince the followers of your competitors that you can provide better business, service or product.

Just by following your competitor's account, those users have already shown an interest in your product. Interaction with them not only increases your number of followers but also enhances the number of qualified leads.

Some of the best tools are available to find out your competitor's followers. One good example is JustUnfollow which gives information about your competitor's followers accounts by name. In fact, you get a detailed list of all your competitor's followers. After getting the list, you can start interacting with your new potential customers by liking or commenting on their photos.

6.   Engage With Popular Instagrammers

One of the best ways to grow your Instagram community is to get your product featured by any popular Instragammer in your field. However, this tactic charges an advertising cost which can be either in the form of payment or by sending products for review. But, the results obtained with the usage of this tool can be certainly dramatic.

To find the most influential accounts in your niche, you can use Instagram's search function which only requires typing in keywords, hashtags and company names. After finding and following a large account, Instagram will provide a list of similar users who can be followed by you to boost your business.

Before connecting with someone, it is always recommended to check the account profile of the person. In most of the cases, you can easily get an idea and know if an account accepts product reviews or sponsored posts. Not only this, but you may also find various users with a note showing their willingness to work with different brands.

In case the users don't specify their engagement with brands, you can simply email them and ask about their take on doing featured reviews or sponsored posts. You can also verify the policies followed by them for working on such options.

The rate of featured reviews or sponsored posts takes various factors into account like audience size and the field to which it's connected. The total cost involved in this comparatively lower than various other online advertising options available nowadays. And the best part is that such partnerships give a guarantee of increased engagement and thus, better business growth options for you.

Converting Followers into Customers – How to Do It?

If you talk about the engagement rate of Instagram, it's certainly the best among all the social networks at present. The image centered attractions help in selling products and showcasing one's business in a much better perspective.

After establishing a large targeted audience and winning their trust and loyalty, the next step to grow your business is to convert your borrowers into buyers. Here is a brief description of the three ways in which you can get started:

1. Stress on Scarcity

Here scarcity is related to demand and supply, and when you show the scarcity of a product, more people show their interest in it. It is most commonly practiced by retailers and marketers who try to attract more customers by emphasizing that product or discounted prices are available only for a limited period of time.

Beverly Hames of Fox & Fawn, the famous company, also accepted that almost 20-40% of daily sales are generated through their audience on Instagram.

2. Keep New Products in Spotlight

Want to spotlight your new products? Instagram can do wonders in this as it is one of the prime channels for direct marketing as well as an amazing platform for showcasing one's new products.

An awesome number of 54,000 followers has been established by Packer Shoes on Instagram. It helps the company in highlighting new and exclusive products as well as driving more business for the company.

3. Showcase Social Proof

Any kind of social proof has always been a powerful psychological phenomenon to win the interest of the customers. In this, people consider actions performed by others as an exemplary behavior for a given situation. Here is one of the most common examples which all of us may have experienced. You always show your preference for a product which has already been recommended by your friends or family members.

As per a research, around 63% of consumers show their preference for purchasing from a site which offers social proof in the form of reviews or product ratings. As a fact, customers tend to trust product reviews almost 12 times more than the product descriptions provided by the customers.

Ball Lies in Your Court – Decision is Yours

Finally, it lies in your hands how you grab the attention of the audience and showcase your products on Instagram. However; the results will always amaze you as it will be a targeted advertising channel which can be trusted for providing a good stream of revenue.

CHAPTER FIVE

SNAPCHAT

If you had only ten seconds to sell your brand, what would you want to show your audience? Snapchat's main function allows users to send photos, videos, and texts that disappear after a length from one to ten seconds. The user can determine the length of the message. Users can send directly to their friends or post to their story. Your story is a series of snaps within a 24-hour span. Marketers are using Snapchat to create a narrative that engages audiences daily. Snapchat is quickly growing in popularity with its largest demographic being in the 18 to 34-year-old age range. As Snapchat continues to grow, your target audience will likely join the network's group of active users.

Content is not saved on Snapchat. The most you'll have is potential or existing customers for one message is within the 24 hours of your story. There is value in having the attention of your consumers, which is what business marketers have gravitated towards.

Snapchat is connected to your phone's address book. When you create an account, it will be linked to the cell phone number that created the account. You can then find friends based on their phone numbers. Snapchat uses a very simple display. There are only three screens. When you first open the app, you are shown the camera. You can swipe down to see your profile statistics, click the top lefthand of the screen to toggle on flash (Flash is available for front and back cameras) and toggle camera view from selfies to front-facing. At the bottom of the main screen, you can tap the circle on the bottom to take a picture or hold it to take a video. Remember, you only have up to 10 seconds!

Onceyou take a photo or record a video, you can add text or draw on top of the picture by using the icons on the top-right hand side of the screen. These will only appear after you've taken the picture or video. On the bottom, you will have options for setting the time others can view your picture, download the photo or video to your phone and send. Be sure to activate filters under your settings. Filters, similar to Instagram's, add to your photos and videos. To activate, click the gear icon in the top right-hand corner of your profile and select *Manage*. Snapchat filters include time, weather, colored filters, speed, reverse your speech, speed up your speech and sometimes special geotagged locations. We will discuss geotag filters later in this chapter.

You can send snaps to individuals or post to your story. Your friends will not receive a notification when you post to your story, but they will receive a notification if you send to them directly. You can see who opens your snaps if sent to an individual, as well as who watches your snaps in a story. You arealso able to see who screenshots your content.

Swipe left for screen one, which shows you snaps you have received from others, as well as the status of snaps you've sent to individuals. On screen one, you can see if people you are messaging have read or seen your message. Swipe right for screen three, which shows you Snapchat stories. As you follow others, you have the option to see their stories. Screen three is a scrolling list of your friends. One of Snapchat's newest features allows for "movie viewing." When you tap to watch someone's story, all snaps from other friends will follow until you swipe the screen off.

One of the easiest ways to grow your Snapchat following is to let your followers on other social networks know that you're on Snapchat. Content posted to Snapchat does not live on forever. Take a screenshot of your Snapchat user profile or download a picture or video that was posted to your story. Share it on social media or include in an email. Snapchat also makes it easy to spread the word. When you swipe down to your profile and select *Add Friends*, you can select *Share Username* to post directly to social media and send an email or text.

The first hurdle to using Snapchat is figuring out what to post. Snapchat's uniqueness is geared towards enabling brands to strengthen their point-of-view with real-time marketing. Does your business host events? Give your audience direct access. Events can be as large as a product launch or as small as someone coming into your office. Remember, people make buying decisions based on emotion. Use Snapchat as an opportunity to build trust and loyalty by giving exclusive looks at the behind-the-scenes of the business. Show off your office and the people you work with. Anything that is unique to your business and your brand will make for interesting content.

Coupled with exclusivity, offer contests and promotions to your Snapchat followers. If you have an online business, offer a promo code for 24 hours via your story. You could also run a contest promotion for users that watch your whole story or build anticipation by asking users to wait for a specific snap to complete a call-to-action. You will strengthen your connection with your Snapchat followers by offering some content only on Snapchat. Thus, you're using Snapchat as an entry point for potential customers to learn more about you.

Who are your key influencers? Perhaps you have a close connection with a local media personality, or you collaborate with another popular company. Use your connection to grow your awareness. Speak with your connection and ask them to take on your Snapchat for a day or a week. If you have an event on a routine basis, you could show it from another perspective. Then, also encourage whoever is using your Snapchat to promote following you on their own social networks. While this is a great way to cross-collaborate, you will want to have a discussion with other users of your profile to ensure they post content that is in line with your brand. It is okay to deviate a little as your collaborator may want to also showcase their brand. But at the core of the agreement, you will want to remain true to your business' brand.

Geotag filtering is a great way to engage users with your brand. As mentioned before, Snapchat is all about the story. One of the ways to maximize exposure of your brand is using geotag filtering for an event or campaign. Snapchat allows you to purchase a filter for a set amount of time in a specific geographic region. You design your own artwork. During the time your filter is enabled and users are in your "geofence," which is the term used to describe your specific geographic region, users can add your filter to their snaps. This paid approach enables you to get an image, campaign name or event in front of new and existing customers. Your brand becomes a part of someone else's story when you invest in geotag filtering. Budweiser sponsors the Made in America Music Festival in Philadelphia each year. Once Snapchat users entered the festival, they were able to add the Budweiser Made in America geotag filter to their snaps. Many users downloaded their photos and reposted on other social networks.

Another popular function of Snapchat is the ability to draw doodles. Using the pencil icon after you take photos or videos, you can be creative and go to town on a drawing. There are Snapchat users who have integrated these drawings into their brand. While they may be selling a product or service that isn't related to art, they use illustration art as a consistent and interesting hook for consumers to connect with. You can also add text and emojis to your images and videos and make them as small or large as you'd like. If your brand has more of a free spirit, then Snapchat is the perfect place to show it.

Snapchat offersusers a sense of urgency that is unique to any other social network. There is an expiration for every snap you send and with interesting content; you can develop a niche audience that will continue to follow your story. Since Snapchat is still growing in popularity, it is likely that its functionality will continue to improve, and new features will become available.

With more than 30 million active users, you should consider how Snapchat can fit in with your brand. With growth, businesses will be able to even better promote their brand.

Best Ways to Use Snapchat for Business

Wondering how to use the latest launched social networking site Snapchat for growing your business and the promotion of your products. Don't worry, it not helps in business growth and product promotion, but also helps in striking a deeper connection with your followers. It can also help you in attaining increased loyalty of the customers, engaged fan following and work a great deal in boosting your brand visibility.

Snapchat can help you build an engaged following, increase loyalty, and boost your brand visibility.

1: Reveal the Backstage Happenings

McDonald showed the world what happens behind the beautifully laid out tables and how its tempting dishes are prepared at the launch of the new bacon clubhouse sandwich.

It was also posted on Twitter which achieved a great fan following. The same philosophy can be applied with Snapchat. You can lure your customers by showing the happenings behind the scenes. Every buyer enjoys knowing the growth story behind your company and also helps in growing your business.

2: Go in Favor of an Account Takeover

The Snapchat campaign launched by the young women's clothing retailer Wet Seal was quickly taken over by a Snapchatter named MsMeghanMakeup.

With over 300,000 followers, Meghan's influence was quickly felt over Wet Seal's campaign. It gave the clothier to 9,000 connections in two weeks and the holiday 'story' got over 250,000 views. The brand also became the winner of the 6th Annual Shorty Awards in which company with the best performance in social media is awarded.

To make your presence felt, you can also support an influential Snapchat user to take over your account. No need to worry if you do not have connections with a huge number of followers as even local authorities with just hundreds or thousands of fans can help to a great extent in improving your Snapchat reach.

3: Sharing Promo Codes

By using Snapchat's instant photo feature, Frozen yogurt chain 16 Handles amassed followers and promoted their frozen treats. Not only this, but they also became the first brand to have used Snapchat for coupon offers.

Learning a good tactic from this, you can also get your followers engaged with Snapchat-exclusive coupon codes or other exclusive promos. If you make it a source of enjoyment for others, nobody can stop your business from growing. So, always try to mingle fun while getting your brand or business promoted.

4: Offer VIP Access

If we look at the past, several weeks were spent in getting photos from New York Fashion Week to reach the desk of consumers. Now, the scene has completely changed as with Snapchat; followers can watch the fashion shows almost instantly.

So, by using the Snapchat feature, you can let your followers enjoy a VIP look at your events and promotions. In fact, they would love it as rarely anyone gets a chance to attend such events personally. It's certainly a simple way to blow new life to established events and present them in a more fascinating manner.

5: Attribute Your Followers

Mobile and online food ordering brand GrubHub launched its first Snapchat campaign in 2013 and also reached until the final round in the 7th Annual Shorty Awards. For this, they showcased their own weekly content and stories collected from various user-generated content, promotions and giveaways.

The brand experienced a 20% increase in the number of its followers after launching the Snapchat giveaway. The campaign also led to its Wall Street debut in a public offering.

So, rise above from making your Snapchat only dedicated to yourself. Post feed about your followers, make them feel valuable and also engage them in the process of content creation for your Snapchat page.

6: Demonstrate Your Product

One of the world's biggest online retailers, Amazon, used Snapchat effectively to give a personality as well as voice to Alexa, which was later launched as the company's female-voiced Echo speaker. By using social media efficiently, Amazon used Snapchat to give a clear view of the product as well as to promote Echo.

This campaign proved successful, and Amazon got 6,100 mentions in merely four hours. So, if you want to promote new products of your brand, you can use Snapchat to offer detailed guidance to the new customers. You can also use snapchat for introducing new products as well as engaging with the potential customers.

7: Do Partnership with Influencers

Doing partnership with an influencer whose fan following base is quite similar to yours can be effectively used for sharing snaps which coincide with your brand's image. It helps in making the task easier as well as in gaining more connections as you get to share more relevant snaps.

8: Focus on Relevant Issues

The famous soap brand Dove was primarily loved by older women until it started engaging younger women using Snapchat. In a campaign launched by Dove, 30 women chatted with psychologists and other ambassadors for a period of half an hour on Snapchat to discuss their views about self-esteem issues in order to help in enhancing the self-images of the young women.

The snaps taken as a result earned the brand 75 conversations and 130,000 views. After this, Dove started giving importance to both the engagement that is of the young women as well as the old women.

It shows how Snapchat can also help in highlighting the real issues faced by us as authenticity plays a pivotal role on this social network.

9: Pay Attention to Exclusive Previews

As per a report published by Business Insider, the famous brand Acura used Snapchat to make customers fascinated for its racecar-like NSX. An exclusive preview of the new car was sent by the automobile manufacturer to its100 followers using Snapchat. Those followers got the 6-second amazing video of the speeding luxury car.

This initiative on Snapchat made Acura named a finalist in the 6th Annual Shorty Awards. Not only were this, but the car also created a lot of interest among the customers and later similar campaigns repeated by the brand on Instagram, Twitter and Vine.

In a similar way, any company can reward its flowers or top customers using Snapchat. Sharing such exclusive information only with a limited number of people always raises the curiosity and can work wonders whether the brand is international or a local one.

10: Do Promotion of Events

iHeartRadio used Snapchat for sharing its iHeartRadio Music Festival. Within two days, the company earned a whopping 340 million impressions with the experiences shared by eager concertgoers. In fact, the festival gained a lot of publicity on Snapchat.

This shows how ephemeral nature of Snapchat makes it a wonderful option for the advertisement of limited time events. So, go ahead and make it a part of your next event to gain maximum publicity.

The above facts have given an amazing set of examples to understand how Snapchat can be effectively used for the growth of one's business or marketing one's products and services. Now, let's discuss in brief a few interesting ways how you can use these tactics in your own Snapchat marketing.

Move Ahead with Snapchat Marketing and Grow your Business

The Snapchat success stories shared above can be an eye opener for many who ignore this social media platform. Whether you are a small or a big brand, here are a few tips which can boost loyalty of your customers with your brand using Snapchat:

Understand the Needs of Your Audience – Knowing your audience is the first step which plays a crucial role in the success of any marketing campaign. By understanding the needs of your audience, you can strike a connection with them easily. The connection part becomes more important on Snapchat where only a few seconds play a pivotal role in making an impression.

Create Unforgettable and Interesting Content – As you get only a few seconds to convey your ideas, the content must be memorable enough to strike a lasting impression. It takes guts to stand out from the crowd, but a positive content always makes the approach successful. Don't be afraid to stand out with positive, brand-building content. You just need to make the public understand the worth of your brand as well as your own importance.

Share Your Personal Experiences – If you are pitching for a faceless brand, it may not be successful on Snapchat as people using Snapchat love to see personal stories. The category of 18-24-year old's mainly shows interest in such brands which has some interesting personal tidbits attached to it.

Follow an Exclusive Approach- An approach different and more beneficial as compared to others always win greater attention. Snapchat gives a lot of preference to coupons, offers and sneak peeks as those are always exclusive. Exclusivity sells well on this platform. Brands like16 Handles and Acura created a higher chance of being viewed by offering exclusive offers.

Maintain Authenticity – Brands with authentic stories always do better on Snapchat as it also reflects the core brand values of a brand. Avoid too much scripting and create a memorable impression with the use of right advertising means.

The usage of Snapchat for promoting one's brand or business can certainly turn the conventional marketing process upside down. Get over the fever of sharing gorgeous product photography and start focusing on genuine snaps.

Yes, in the beginning, it may take a little time, but Snapchat can prove an amazing way to market your brand.

CHAPTER SIX

LINKEDIN

Throughout this chapter, we are going to deal with an extraordinarily well developed page. LinkedIn is a business-oriented social networking site. It was founded in December 2002 and was launched on May 5 of the following year. At the time of its launch, it was a groundbreaking idea to connect work professionals from around the world via one social network. But the idea remained, grew and developed to unimaginable boundaries. As of this writing, LinkedIn has more than 433 million accounts and counting. It is based in the United States, and it is available in 24 languages. From 2015 onward, most of the site's income came from advertising and from access to information on its users to send to recruiters and/or sales professionals.

Without any doubt, LinkedIn is the best choice when hiring professionals. There are some good alternative sites but you will not regret joining LinkedIn. It is a tool for navigating through professional waters, and its design and functionality create a positive effect for both employees and employers alike. It is a new way to hire young and talented people who update their profiles along with their experience and education. Employees can make references, find new working experiences, and managers are able to find candidates, and reach out to them directly through InMail. This offers a direct engagement which is more powerful, and an excellent way to show their interests in properly qualified candidates who would fit their needs.

Certainly, this is a good opportunity to train and educate employees and hire professionals. Users search the market for the terms that are suitable for their working skills. Everyone should be encouraged to join groups and raise their brand awareness to attract people who can help them make their brand better in any possible way. This works through contacts, which are very important in the business world.

- **Make a profile and make a profit**

You should make the most out of your company page or profile by accenting the keywords that other sides use during their search. If you decide just to post about your company content and hope for the best, then you are not using it right. It is hopeless. Try to engage more by getting the staff involved and not just hoping for success. If you own the company and you want to hire, provide job seekers with pieces of information they want and need to know about you as a potential future employer: what you ask for, what you offer, what your mission is, your vision, values and benefit packages. Your content should be short but informative. Design your engaging page in a way that is easy for candidates to navigate in order to encourage their interest in the company.

The basic functions of LinkedIn allow all users, employees and employers, to make connections to each other in the same way other social networks do, except that these connections represent professional relationships. You, as a user, are able to invite anyone you choose whether or not they already use a site. Upon joining, they become your connection. In spite of this, if the invited person clicks the option "I don't know" or "spam" this acts like a negative point for the inviter. Even worse, if your invitations get rejected too many times your account may be restricted or even closed. Be careful. But if you do everything else right, you shouldn't be worried.

There are many different kinds of connections on LinkedIn:

- Acquiring introductions to the connections of connections (which are called *second-degree connections*), and connections of second-degree connections (called *third-degree connections*). Users can look for second-degree connections, for example, a person who works at a specific company they are interested in, and then request a particular first-degree connection in common for an introduction.

- Users can also look for jobs, for people, and for business opportunities according to the recommendation of a user in their contact network.

- Employers can file job requests and seek out potential candidates and reach them easily according to their working skills and connections.

- Those users who seek the job are able to review the profile of hiring managers and learn which of their current contacts can introduce them.

- Al users can post their photos as a way of identification.

- Job seekers can save or bookmark jobs that they are interested in and would like to apply for.

- All users can "like" and "congratulate" each other's updates, for example, new employments.

However, there are some guidelines listed below that you want to know when setting up a profile on LinkedIn.

1. Be careful not to bother others

For example, when you're updating your profile, go to edit mode, then to your privacy controls, turn off activity broadcasts and change your settings in "select who can see your activity feed" to "only you." This way the little changes you make in your profile won't annoy your contacts who will otherwise be alerted every time you make those changes. Imagine that you received tons of notifications ever day from someone who can't really decide on anything.

2. Seize an opportunity

Try to find and join groups that will let you connect with those in your target audience but are not necessarily your contacts. Invite them to join your network, exchange opinions and reach out for opportunities for job improvement. In order to do so, you are not required to upgrade your profile to Premium. Do not put a limit on the number of groups you join. Join any group you think is related to your area of expertise and any group that can make a change for you, either in a professional aspect or within other aspects of your identity. This also provides access to more people who could matter to your brand. In addition, others can learn about your brand just by looking at your groups. Pick the groups that are active and have a lot of members.

3. Repeat what you want to be known about you

Write down your top five strengths for which you want to be recognized, and repeatedly present them in your profile. Describe your proficiency in your summary as well as in numerous knowledge and skill descriptions. This will be helpful for the right audience to find you. Also, you will know at all times what principles you should satisfy. It will become your mantra.

4. Be economical with your time

Try to reuse and/or repurpose the content you have available. This may also amplify your message and deliver your brand consistency. Communicating several forms of the same content in an individual way helps strengthen your message about the brand. Adapt your blog posts to include activity updates and embed articles in your profile.

5. Make new connections

You may want to overlook LinkedIn's advice about only accepting requests for connections from people you know. It doesn't assist you in any case since you may not be found at all. LinkedIn's search options will favor those who are in your network. This means that when people are looking at your offers, the findings of their searches are primarily displayed with first level connections, then second level connections, and so on.

6. Voice your opinion

It would be good for your success to include your point of view (POV) into your profile summary and experience if and where appropriate. Join those groups where it is welcomed to express your POV for your area of expertise. It's a fantastic way to distinguish yourself on the market.

7. Organize your profile

Your profile is not your resume or CV. Try to write it as though you are simply talking to someone. Be creative so you stand out; add your personality to it. With these simple changes, you can be sympathetic to your potential employers. Don't be afraid to reorder the content of your profile. List what you believe is important and choose which strengths to focus on. Feel free to let people know your ideals and passions. But don't assume you need to enter every single detail of every job you have ever had. You are trying to be irresistible, not desperate. In your summary, discuss what you love to do outside of work. Just like I said – you are talking to someone, and you want them to know you and like you.

CHAPTER SEVEN

PINTEREST

Another great way to promote your business is Pinterest, and as it says, it is the world's catalog of ideas. It really is, and you can find almost anything from DIY to travel sites. It was founded by Ben Silbermann, Paul Sciarra and Evan Sharp in December 2009, and the site launched as a closed beta in March of the next year. The site continued to successfully operate in invitation-only open beta. One of the founders, Silbermann, said he personally contacted the site's first 5,000 users and offered his personal phone number and to even meet with some of its users in person.

By December 2011, Pinterest became one of the top 10 largest social network services with a total of 11 million visits per week. In that same month, the company was chosen by TechCrunch as the best new startup company of 2011. A month later, comScore noted the site had 11.7 million unique users. This made it the fastest site in history to break the 10 million unique visitor point. In March 2012, Pinterest presented an updated version of its terms of service that removed the policy that gave them the right to sell the content of its users. Soon, the site became the third largest social network, behind Facebook and Twitter, in the United States in 2012.

In June 2015, Pinterest introduced "buyable pins". These were called Rich Pins, and these pins have more information than a normal link. There's a new button that lets the user buy things straight from the users that utilize this button. Users are able to see prices and select a particular product, choose the color or size, and whatever that specific item includes, and then press the button to buy the product. Later that year, in December 2015, Pinterest launched a new option for its users. This time, they were able to monitor price changes or sales on buyable pins. Users receive an in-app notification and an email about the price drop, which can help them make the purchase. This is the page that went a step further and really created the possibility for small brands to directly sell to their potential customers.

In August 2016, Pinterest launched a video player that allows users and brands to upload and store videos of any length directly to the site.

It is a website which offers free registration for its users. You can connect your Pinterest account with your Facebook profile and share videos and images through so called pins, and then save them, sort them, and present them to others, or keep them for yourself in collections known as pinboards. Pinterest works as a personalized media platform. Users can pick the content of their news feed according to their interests, in a similar way hashtags work for Instagram or Twitter. Users are able to save, or pin any particular image or video seen on Pinterest or any other page or blog and upload it to one of their own boards by using the "Pin It" button. There are some websites that are connected with Pinterest and include red and white pins on their images or videos. This allows Pinterest users to pin them directly on their chosen board. Pinboards are usually named and organized by a key figure of the board. Through this, users can personalize their profile and experience with Pinterest, which can help them interact with other like-minded members. These pinboards also work in a certain way as bookmarks on your web browser. "I like this. I'll save it for later!" You can do this on a public or private pinboard.

Pinterest also has the option of sharing a pin with other Pinterest users, but it also allows you to send a pin to an email account through the "Send" button.

There are several ways to set up a new Pinterest account. Hypothetical users could either get an invite from a registered friend via email or some other social network or send the request to join to the Pinterest website directly. In August 2012, Pinterest no longer needed a request or an invite to join the site, and today everyone can be a part of this growing family. When a user pins or re-pins an image or a video to their pinboard, they have the option of notifying their Facebook friends and/or Twitter followers. This can be easily managed on the settings page.

For Pinterest users as well as page guests, there are four main sections to browse at the moment, and they are sorted by names: Everything, Videos, Popular, and Gifts. It is also important to note that there is the Pinterest iPhone application as well as an Android application, available through the App Store or Play Store, which makes it easier for both current and future users to connect with this interesting platform.

The website was proven to be especially popular among women. According to research in 2012, 70% of the female audience in the United States accessed the website through the computer and the average user spent 90 minutes per month on Pinterest. The most popular categories you can find on Pinterest up to this day are DIY & crafts, food & drink, women's clothing, home decor, and travel.

However, having a certain strategy for your Pinterest activities will help you achieve better results. Don't feel like it is a recipe, but it will certainly help you connect with others out there who have the same interest as you do.

1. Create pinboards that include keywords in your title

Pinterest has terrific search capabilities; try it yourself, you will be amazed. You may try using keywords in your board titles in order to bring even more people to your online backyard and learn about your business. Be sure to select a category for each pinboard and choose the option for Pinterest to suggest your board as well. This way you will be found much quicker and easier. And in that case, don't put your pinboard on private.

2. Describe your ideas

Once more, use keywords in your description as well. Keep in mind that people can tweet or share your pins via Facebook. What you write as the pin description becomes the tweet so keep it brief, appealing, and relevant.

3. Choose vertical images to make the most of your real estate

Pinterest images should be long and narrow in order to take up the greatest amount of visual space. Note what your favorite pins have in common and then apply it to your images. You will be able to recognize what types of images are repinned and shared. Most users do not include a big image but have one that pins with every post. So have a pinnable image on each post that you share.

5. Embed pins on your blog and share the pins on other social media networks

Embedding pins on your blog is a simple and cool way to get more repins. Just create an embed code on your Pinterest site. Tweet your pin or share them on your other social networks where you believe they are relevant.

6. Rich pins

According to Pinterest, there are five types of Rich Pins at the moment: movie, recipe, article, product, and place. You can advertise almost everything, and almost everything can be bought. Find your chosen Rich Pins and apply to get them. If you're not skilled, ask your developer or site owner to help you get what you are looking for.

7. Create mutual pinboards

Collaborative boards can help you connect with a new group of interested users and allow your pins to be seen by a larger audience. No need to be careful about which boards to join since all the pins will show up on your Pinterest as well. If you are the owner of the group board, you may select the cover photo of your collaborative board.

CHAPTER EIGHT

FLICKR

Flickr began as a series of features in a massive multiplayer online game, Game Neverending. This game was created by a married couple from Canada, developers Steward Butterfield and Caterina Fake, and developer Jason Classon. However, when the game shut down, the firm launched Flickr as a separate site. It quickly became popular, creating a considerable user base and drawing the attention of industry publications and firms. Butterfield's existing firm, called Ludicorp, was quickly bought by Yahoo in 2005. This happened only a year after launch and Yahoo bought Ludicorp for $35 million. This meant changes! Yahoo improved storage limits for users, but, as some critics conclude, fell short when it came to developing the existing social community. This meant leaving the area open for other social media such as Facebook and Instagram to take social market share. Despite the fact that the integration with Yahoo had many positive sides including enabling all registered users to use Flickr, and helped Flickr's user base to grow, the transition likely cost Yahoo the commitment of Flickr's extremely active users from an early period. They also came across difficulties with mobile engagement since Yahoo Mobile's Flickr functionality was badly designed and made only for already existing users.

Today, Flickr is one of the best photo-sharing platforms, and its direct competitors include Instagram, Photobucket, Shutterfly, SmugMug, Picasa, Kodak Gallery, Pinterest, and Snapfish in the photo-sharing area; and Facebook, Google+, Tumblr, and Pheed in the social space. Still, Flickr has an enormous database of organized photos, and has a user base of 92 million and growing.

Flickr was initially designed as part of an MMOG to improve the experience of its users, and with this in mind, was created for users to organize and stock photos. It also encouraged connections with each other's photo content. Up to this day, the purpose has remained unchanged. Free account users get a Terabyte (TB) of storage. This is more than enough, and it is brilliant for archiving photos, particularly for amateur and professional photographers, in case they might want to put away uncompressed files for their later in-depth photo editing. On the other hand, Flickr still has tools of a social network, for example, the ability to like the content, make a comment on it, and even share it, as well as to create and join groups built around a common interest. Like Instagram, Flickr also has mobile applications for iOS and Android operating systems.

Flickr is suitable for sharing your photos, organizing them, presenting both your skills and artistic eye, and, of course, archiving and saving those you wouldn't want to be forgotten. It is perfect for photographers, for marketing initiatives and for creative souls. You may organize photos with no trouble, edit them, tag their geographical location, and access them from computers or mobile phones.

Flickr can be effortlessly incorporated into content management systems (CMS), such as WordPress or Drupal, if you want to display your photo collection on your blog or website. You can decide who can access which photos, set up your privacy controls, as well as turn on filters in order to categorize the content which is uploaded and/or searched for. Photos uploaded on Flickr can also be shared on your Facebook, Twitter, Tumblr or other social media accounts without any problems. The free TB of storage is significantly more than the storage space offered by any other photo sharing sites, and obviously, you can use it to download photos of any size. Just for comparison, Google, for instance, offers unlimited space to download files that have a maximum size of 2,048 pixels. Then again, it charges $50.00 per month for a TB with unlimited download size. Flickr offers three different accounts: Free with 1 TB of storage, Doublr, which offers 2 TBs of storage, as its name says, and Pro accounts which offer you unlimited storage.

Furthermore, its social part of the network allows you to expand your brand online, show your strengths, present your work, build brand awareness, find partners or customers, and enhance SEO. It has over 10 million Groups to join, each based on mutual interest. Therefore, Flickr mail allows you to connect with other users. The Explore link takes you to the vast gallery of Flickr photos. Photos selected here are usually unique or popular or even both. Flickr's mobile application lets you shoot and edit short videos, up to 30 seconds, which makes it a direct challenge to Vine and Instagram.

By the way, it is very important to note that Flickr claims no ownership rights to the photos that are being uploaded onto its site, which is a popular policy among other photo-sharing sites.

To create your Flickr account, you need to have or set up a Yahoo account. Both are free and simple. When you visit Yahoo, pick Flickr on the top of the page and then click Sign Up on the next page. You may be asked for some personal information on the following page. But just like with any social network, you create your username, ideally a name closely related to your business brand. Once you sign in you are ready to upload and arrange photos. You may need to consider a few things before you start uploading your photos:

In what order are you going to organize your photos? What albums, collections, and tags will you need to include, how will you figure out the best options for other viewers, and consider the way your photos are going to be arranged in a user-friendly manner? Are you going to give permission to other users to have access and use the photos? Are your photos going to be high quality and unique? Flickr users appreciate posts that are both of high quality and unique. Therefore you may want to reconsider uploading your randomly taken smartphone shots. Stay professional.

- **How to use Flickr for business**

Even though it is sometimes neglected as a way to present and offer your business skills, or forgotten, unlike other social media tools, Flickr offers many benefits and advantages, including, as already mentioned, displaying and archiving photos.

Many business companies struggle with storing their digital photo collections. Photos usually take a lot of server space for such businesses, considering the file format and quality. A Flickr Pro account costs $50.00 a year and offers unlimited server space. On the plus side, Flickr tools, for example, Organizer, offers an easy and practical labeling, categorizing, and tagging of your photos, either individually or in bulk, for posterity.

It allows users to decide whether or not their photos are going to be publicly visible. Possible integration with WordPress is flawless; other CMS' can present Flickr content on webpages as well. Even if your content cannot be shown automatically, you can always add a link to your Flickr photo collection online. Additional to the above mentioned uses, Flickr can be a terrific site to find stock photos you can use to display on your website, if the author allows, of course, and in a lot of situations it is much cheaper than stock photos offered on stock photography sites.

1 TB of storage space can be used to upload videos as well. They can be either shot with Flickr tools or others. Flickr does not include pop-up advertisements on videos you decide to present publicly on Pro accounts. You are capable of uploading high definition videos of up to 1 GB each and up to 3 minutes.

- **Extend your reach and visibility**

By uploading your photos on Flickr you are not only organizing them, saving them or sharing them with others on existing social networks, you can also contact fellow Flickr users, share your impressions by leaving a comment on photos, learn a few tricks on exposure or Photoshop use. You can learn about how something is made, and demonstrate your knowledge of your field. A million photos are shared each day on the site which means that Flickr's users are highly active and engaged, which is a bonus for you as well.

Flickr also provides the option for visitors to print out photobooks from albums and/or collections of photos, which can be helpful in spreading the word about your product or service, or rather, a photo of your talent or business.

- **Expand your network**

Flickr may not be near the publicity that Facebook or Twitter can offer in terms of social network reach. However, since it is a part of a free service to Yahoo customers, it still has an impressive number of registered users. You can invite your friends to join by clicking the link under Contacts. You can import your email contacts database to Flickr and check which members you know are already on Flickr, and send an invitation to those who are not. Just like with any other social network, you can join groups and connect with other Flickr users to expand your contact list. From these foundations, you can build your brand awareness, make sales leads, and control product and market research.

Try to be visible by optimizing your photos, making tags and titles to appear high in search results. Find, ask for or make pictures of happy and joyful consumers while using your product. Interestingly enough others may find it worthy of their trust and, therefore, engage more, buy your products or share it on some of their social media networks. Even one share can do you more good than harm.

- **What you need to do on Flickr**

Organize and upload photos in such a way that your best photos are shown last. This way your best photographs are going to show up first. If you want to pique the interest of the audience in some of your initiatives or events do upload photos in real-time, as this may create discussions and spread the word even more. And yes, try to make great photos, they attract more viewers and potential contacts. Create groups that are relevant to your target audience and your customers. Share the content which is of interest to them. There is an option to create Flickr Badges, so you make them, embed them on your website and/or blog to create a direct link to your photos. Use Flickr to share photos on Facebook, Twitter, and Tumblr. This way they will keep the quality that may become distorted when uploading them directly to one of the aforementioned networks. Regularly make a review of your visits and assess your data by enabling stats.

1. **Interestingness**

This may sound like "Alice in Wonderland" but Flickr created this word for a developed patented feature called

"Interestingness". This organizes your photographs according to an algorithm which observes views, comments, favorites and the speed by which these are collected. Every day a collection of the photos with the highest Interestingness are featured on Explore pages. This is an awesome space to check out new and creative stuff.

One more thing that can help you make your photos visible to a larger extent is placing your photos on a map to mark the actual location in which they were taken. It is good to know that photos which are placed high in Interestingness are highlighted on local Yahoo! news pages serving those particular geographical areas. Besides, you can look through a map of the places you want to visit in order to view photos taken there and pick up ideas on what to shoot, where and when.

2. Give the information on the tools you use

Flickr users would be grateful to know what camera and what settings you used to make that mind-blowing photo they liked so much. You can enter this when uploading a new photo or edit under the More Properties link. This could be a great way to help others build their photography knowledge, and it will certainly mean an upvote.

Interestingly, Flickr tracks the number of photos taken on hundreds of brands of digital cameras every day. This may be a good marketing strategy for camera brands so you can check out a camera's capabilities before potentially buying one. On the other hand, it may also assist you to assure yourself that your camera is not as bad as you think and that it is able to take pictures of similar quality. Also, there are groups dedicated to various categories, and their members will hopefully be interested in sharing their knowledge about particular types of photography. Don't be afraid to ask.

There are some occasional opportunities that you need to seize. Many other companies, web creators and publishers look for materials for themselves. Many Flickr members have found a way to sell or feature their photos in magazines, books and web sites. This may seem slightly impossible for you. In the vast ocean of amazing photographs, why would someone pick you? It happens that if you follow the rules of Flickr – check Flickr, learn something, go out there, be creative, shoot the perfect photo, upload it as it was said, and reach out to the audience, you will be amazed by the result. Even if you don't succeed the first time, follow the comments of professional photographers who may have left the tip for you under the photo, and try again, and again. You will get better.

Plus, many groups have competitions in which members of that particular group vote on posts in a variety of contests.

Even some organizations have agreed with Flickr to move their competitions onto this photo sharing site, such as Nikon, Hewlett-Packard and Ford. They have established groups on Flickr to acquire photos they could potentially use in their marketing campaigns.

3. **Avoid the hard sell in every possible case**

Even though we may advertise our skills there, don't ever post something that looks or feels like an advertisement. Your goal is to find a way to get closer to your customers and not make them run away from your annoying advertisements. It is not an online store; you can manage that elsewhere. It is just an online shopping window. You look around, see what you like, and try to find the way to get it, to get the professionals behind the product, and to learn about the brand itself. That doesn't mean you need to withdraw your products completely from your Flickr account. Use the platform to get the audience involved and base it, rather, around their experience and knowledge, instead of your own marketing skills.

4. **Incorporate Your Flickr link into everything you're doing on the Web**

Go ahead and advertise Flickr. In order to get all the values and see all the positive sides of Flickr, you have to connect it with other platforms you are using. Tell your customers to visit, to explore, and encourage them with a sneak peek preview on your web page or your blog or another social network. Give them information on things they want to know while searching the web. Let them decide if they want to interact with you and give them the reasons why they should.

At the same time, be sure that you're using each social network to the max and in all the glory they can offer. If you have both a YouTube channel and Flickr page, feel free to post videos on Flickr. Nevertheless, keep it focused on photos since it is the original purpose of the page. So don't exaggerate with unnecessary materials. Flickr is all about creative high quality photos, so don't try to change it.

Also if you want to you can upload your photos on a Creative Commons license so people can use them for their purposes. Every time that someone shares your content, that's a bonus for you and your work. You're probably not a professional photography agency that is trying to protect its valuable photos. If you feel particularly anxious about other people stealing your work, use small watermarks somewhere on your photos.

CHAPTER NINE

YOUTUBE

When someone mentions social media networks in terms of business tools not many people think of YouTube. It is indeed a video platform, and it may not initially look like it is a suitable platform for marketing, but now that comments on YouTube are tied to Google+, it became better than ever before. Creating and uploading video content on YouTube is a fantastic method of increasing the visibility and reliability of your brand. YouTube was founded by former employees of PayPal - Chad Hurley, Steve Chen, and Jawed Karim. YouTube also began its path to the stars as a startup idea in 2005.

It had many ups and downs as a company, but today it one of the most visited sites around the world. The first YouTube video, named *"Me at the zoo"* was uploaded on April 23, 2005. The video that first reached one million views in September 2005 was a Nike advertisement featuring Ronaldinho. The site officially launched in December 2005, and by that time the site was getting 8 million views per day.

With every day the page grew, and more and more videos were being uploaded. In 2014 YouTube claimed that 300 hours of new videos were being uploaded to the site each minute. This was unimaginable just a few years earlier. Now YouTube allows high quality videos, live streaming, 3D, **360° videos, managing your profiles, partnership with video creators and much more.** YouTube allows the uploading of videos in most container formats. It also allows 3GP, meaning videos can be uploaded from mobile phones. This makes it easier for you if you decide to advertise your brand on YouTube. While other networks are trying to incorporate videos into their photo-sharing sites, YouTube still sticks to what it does best. From a small apartment over a restaurant to large office headquarters, YouTube proves that nothing is impossible.

There is no need to go into details about how to present this media. You all know how to use YouTube, and you know what it can offer, but still there are some tips you need to know in order to present your brand properly. You set up an account, which is joined with your Google account. Create a channel and make a short video about your brand and yourself and tell the viewers what to expect and try to intrigue them. Your videos should really have a purpose. This is going to work for you if you have design skills you want to present or some artistic talent for which you can record the creation.

1. Be active

YouTube channels with the greatest popularity are those that have consistently updated content. If you decide to use video as a tool for advertising your brand, you will have to make and upload a lot of videos. And you can do it in plenty of ways. For example, through webcasts and webinars that can be broken up and posted in a series. You can make short tutorials or explainer videos and product demonstrations. Be active in your comments as well. People will rate your videos and leave comments. Respond to the feedbacks as soon as possible and be professional; it is not your personal site, but your brand's window to the world.

2. Customize your channel

Show what it is really about, so it can be visible from plain sight. It will be great if it doesn't look like every other YouTube page. Add some colors, images, links, relevant information and possibly use your logo, particular color palette, tone, and slogans so that viewers associate the video with your business. Encourage the viewers to subscribe and get notified whenever you upload a new video.

3. Think through your titles

People usually search YouTube the same way they do on Google, so use keywords and phrases that describe what they might be looking for. If you need a description for a video, there is a place for that as well. Describe your video in a few short sentences including your top keywords and add a link to your brand's website or blog for people who want to know more about it.

The rest you should leave to viewers and potential customers. Your videos can easily be shared on any network and therefore, you can reach more visibility than you had hoped for. Think through if you have something to offer to YouTube since it is different from other social media networks. Admit if you have not. Don't just leave it on its own and expect to be discovered. It doesn't just happen overnight. Like everything else it needs to be cherished and groomed.

4. Engage With The Audience

Probably the most important aspect of social media and what makes it different from all other media is the fact that you get to see your users' comments and feedback in real time. The moment you post a new YouTube video, your customers can comment and like your video and share it on their social media channels such as Facebook or Twitter.

Having one of your videos go viral on social media can be worth thousands of dollars in completely free marketing and some companies have dedicated themselves to creating YouTube campaigns that will get real exposure. Old Spice was one of the companies who utilized YouTube in a very innovative way, creating videos that answered their customer's social media comments and went absolutely viral for a while, giving the company huge exposure with next to nothing spent in the marketing budget.

If we take into consideration the amount of money some brands are spending on marketing their products, there is no doubt that successful YouTube campaigns can save you large amounts of cash and make your brand huge at the same time. The real trick to YouTube exposure is certainly communication and interaction with the audience, and all the marketing industry insiders know this.

Long gone are the days of simply throwing a TV ad out there and hoping something good comes out of it. Today, the trick is in interaction, which means keeping track of what your customers are commenting, as even those comments that may seem like trolling can help you get more exposure if you play your cards right.

For instance, if there is a joke that keeps recurring in the comments section of your YouTube videos, why not use this to your advantage, create a video that uses this joke as its theme and make your audience absolutely love your brand because you took the joke in jest, instead of going on the defense. The truth is that today's audience loves the hype and stuff that can go viral, so give them what they want.

What's more, the YouTube comments section is a great place to give your customers some great support without them even asking for it. It won't cost you too much to have one customer support agent go through the YouTube comments on a regular basis and leave replies wherever they can to help the customers out. If your customers need some help or seem confused, the agent can help them and if they are simply commenting on the product they can be interacted with, which can often lead to better customer satisfaction and possibly some great exposure. A happy customer is more likely to recommend you to people and share your content on their social media, which again translates to free marketing.

Generally speaking, we could say that interaction with the customers via social media is key to increse brand awareness and YouTube is certainly one where interaction will lead to great results. All the big brands are doing it and for a small brand, it may have even more value as just a few dedicated customers may be enough to significantly increase brand awareness among the general public.

CHAPTER TEN

MEASURING YOUR SUCCESS

There are many ways to monitor the success of a brand. You can track metrics on new followers, engagement, impressions and keyword mentions. Most social networks will generate reports for you with this information. Just looking at how many new followers you have each month is not enough. Drill down deeper to see which posts caused the audience growth. Engagement measures how many followers are taking the extra step to interact with your content. Impressions are how many times someone sees your content. To calculate your engagement rate, divide the number of engagements by the number of impressions. Keyword mentions help you gain insight into an individual campaign. If you are actively promoting users to use a specific keyword and no one is, then you can conclude your campaign was a fail and reevaluate your strategy.

Remember the importance of emotions when promoting your brand. As consumers have an emotional response, businesses have better engaged their audience. While much of what you will measure to determine your success will focus on the numbers or quantitative data, you can also look at sentiment. Most social networks have a feature for consumers to contact you. Tools such as Google Alerts, Klout, Social Mention and Simply Measured can help you more easily monitor what people are saying about you. Look at the emotion behind posts about you. Are what people say about you positive or negative? Use sentiment as a barometer for your social media branding strategy.

Once again, play the card of emotions. Satisfied customers will surely post photos or a status. Unfortunately, unsatisfied customers will too, although in a negative context. Try to grant them their wishes and hopes of your brand. Upload positive testimonials you have received from your customers; they will feel special and so will you. They will be glad if you use their words or upload their photo using your product, and others may join in your game.

Other ways to measure your social media efforts are reach, site traffic, leads generated and revenue generated. Reach is the amount of people who received impressions on a Page post. While impressions reveal how many times people saw your post, reach will show you unique numbers. Your reach will be lower than impressions. Site traffic will show you how many people moved from your social media page or post to your website. Tools like Google Analytics allow you to look at the backend of your website and discover how someone landed on your main page. You can see if they clicked on a link or if they googled you. This is valuable insight when measuring brand awareness.

Leads generated are the number of emails, addresses or phone numbers collected. Any means of contacting someone to further showcaseyour brand is lead generated. With paid advertising, you're able to generate leads and collect data automatically. With organic posts, refer users to a form on a landing page. The number of completed forms will be your metric. Lastly, revenue generated is the number of dollars you receive as a result of your social media efforts. Similar to leads generated, if you're running a paid promotion on social media, that is encouraging users to book a paid appointment with you or purchase a product, then the data is collected by the website. However, revenue generated becomes trickier to track from organic posts.

Having a dedicated landing page is the cleanest way to gather metrics. Landing pages have unique URLs and are not available for the general public to find using a search engine. If you have a public page on your website available, and you're promoting that same link to your social media following, then you aren't able to see the traction your organic social media posts are making. You can use Google Analytics or another web analytic platform, to see how someone arrived on your page. If you use tracking links like ow.ly and bit.ly, then you can see how many clicks to a revenue-generating landing page received.

When you begin tracking your social media metrics, you will need to develop a method for keeping the numbers organized. An excel spreadsheet should do when you first begin. Create sheets for each social network. You will want to monitor on a routine basis. This could be weekly, monthly, or quarterly. If you wait any longer than a quarter to measure your social media, you probably aren't doing a good job maximizing your brand! Put dates in the row cells going across the top and your metrics in the first column. Each month, go down the column recording: number of new followers, comments, likes, shares, and clicks. If you set up any landing pages, be sure to track activity on the landing pages and the referral source, so you know which platform resulted in conversions.

If you're distributing content with the intent to raise brand awareness, the best way to ensure you're on track with your goal is to monitor and measure. Social media marketing provides a huge benefit to business owners, but if you're not maximizing your potential on each network, then you are not maximizing your brand.

You must be thinking how to measure your brand's success on social media. No need to worry for that as there are a number of highly effective tools, some even dedicated to particular social media platforms to measure the success.

You must be able to understand the way the market works and how your brand is going to succeed and develop, and in particular, what audience you are trying to reach on each social network. It is free as far as money, but you're investing your time. Don't let it be spent in waste. Inform yourself about the things you think you need to know for this project. You don't need a person who is going to promote your brand for you. Actually, you do, and those are called Facebook friends, Twitter and Instagram followers, and Flickr contacts. So your customers are also your advertisers – remember Starbucks from the beginning of the story. That is how you do it properly.

On a daily basis, millions of texts, photos and videos are posted on various social media platforms. Some post for personal engagements and others try to make business engagements through it. Now, the question arises, how will your business make a strong impact amid so much noise? Also, how to know if your efforts are reaching your target audience?

Various tools are offered by social media sites to keep a check on one's success. Here's a brief description of the tools which can be used to ensure if the social media tools used are really effective for your marketing:

- **Instagram Business Tools**

A new variety of tools and campaign data to work on real time basis was recently launched by Instagram. It gives you a detailed understanding of the performance of your content or the marketing efforts of your business on social networking sites. The image-based social media site provides detailed information on frequency, reach and impressions of your audience to give you a clear picture of the level of engagement with your audience. With this, you get an idea about the kinds of images more loved by your followers, and it would encourage you to post more content based on the same pattern to maintain future engagement with your audience.

- **Facebook Insights**

With the help of Facebook Insights, you can easily identify page visits, likes, comments and shares. With it, you can also get to know about the unlikes and hidden posts as well. There is a Definitive Guide to Using Facebook Insights available which provides all the details about using this tool and understanding the real stats of your success. You can even add up to 5 pages you want to track and compare the performance of your page with similar pages on Facebook. It will present a total number of likes, the number of likes in a previous week, how many posts were uploaded in that week and the engagement of that week. You can also observe the actions of the page – people who clicked on your action buttons trying to find your address, website or phone number.

- **Crowdbooster**

Crowdbooster offers wonderful social media optimization by combining analytics and recommendations. This web-based application gives a clear understanding of your performance on a range of social media platforms, and also guides how to boost your online influence and strike better engagement with your customers.

With the help of recommendations, you get an opportunity to schedule tweets or posts at the most appropriate time and create more relevant content as per the performance shown by the previous content.

Not only this, but you can also use this platform for responding to missed tweets as well as for crossing posts between social networks. At present, Crowdbooster provides services to measure Twitter and Facebook usage as well. Analytics are effectively used for measuring retweets, impressions, clicks, mentions, likes, replies and comments. On the whole, this tool can help businesses track their followers and fan growth over time which will help in easy identification of frequent commenters or key influencers.

- **Twitter Analytics**

Twitter, the social marketing giant, also offers an updated analytic dashboard though it is specifically available only for Twitter Card publishers, marketers and verified users on the site. The dashboard gives a clear picture of the number of impressions, retweets for each tweet and one's favorites on the site. It also tells the number of times a site visitor has clicked on the tweeter's profile. The best part is that tweet metrics are updated in real time. Using a CSV export tool, you can even check the data up to 3,200 tweets including a breakdown of all tweet impressions. It helps in identifying the tweets attracting the most engagement with audiences on a real time basis. By this, one can easily judge the Twitter strategies which have proved most effective for your marketing efforts.

- **Hootsuite Analytics/UberVu**

Hootsuite has emerged as a quite effective tool as it is a combination of analytics and social media optimization recommendations. The best part is that this tool offers a mobile app as well which can be used for checking one's social media influence from anywhere.

Hootsuite expanded its analytical offerings after acquiring UberVu recently. The UberVu allows you to check the location of your social profile growth and judge the increase in brand sentiment on the basis of social media posts. Not only this, likes, clicks and retweets can also be measured to identify the content which resonates best with your audience. This tools also tells you about spikes around keywords which helps you in responding quickly and effectively while a topic is still trending. The key influencers or customers can also be identified with this tool while they talk about your company or product and share their views.

- **Viralheat**

Viralheat has proved to be highly effective in analyzing over 600 data points which provide information on social media trends. It includes all the social media network giants like Facebook, Pinterest, Twitter, videos, blogs and websites. Viralheat also helps in identifying relevant keywords which can be used for making one's marketing goal stronger.

Sentimental trend reporting is also done by this tool which can help you to know how a particular content goes down your target audience. It also efficiently identifies high activity times, filter mentions, response times, trending content by geographic region. You can get to know about the latest trends for your brand and can filter the best based on the needs of your brand and the interest of the target audience.

It has been noticed that people who are not that tech savvy are afraid of using social media platforms, especially for business purposes as they think that their inefficiency in the usage of tools deter them from taking help of social media giants.

However, it is not that complicated as thought by non-technical people. In fact, anyone holds the ability to master social media platforms for growing one's business with just a little keenness about different tools and give some time to practice.

1. Take Help of an Expert

Sometimes, our confidence in thinking that we will be able to manage everything on our own can prove fatal in gaining long term returns. Though we are smart enough and can even work more than 70 hours a week, there are many other things which a person still needs to learn and master over. Social media is not that difficult to gain mastery, but it certainly needs a significant time to be spent on it if one's business expectations and growth are related to it. If you really want to gain excellence in your business with social media campaigns, and you think you can neither devote so much time, nor you have that expertise, it is always better to hire a consultant who can provide optimum help. It has been proven time and again how effective a consultant can be in helping you to manage your time, money, process as well as the deliverables.

2. Start the Journey with Popular Social Media Platforms

Some of the most popular social media platforms nowadays include Twitter, Facebook, Instagram, Snapchat and Linkedin. Even if you are a beginner, setting up an account on these platforms is quite simple which doesn't need any kind of expertise. You just need to fill a few details which generally ask for giving your name, email address, phone number and physical address.

The most important thing is to maintain patience if you are just a beginner in using social media platforms for the promotion of your business. It may also be possible that you don't get even a single follower on day 1. However, you needn't lose your confidence and keep working on achieving your goals.

A few points you need to pay attention while creating your profile or about page is that you must be highly professional in it. Sites like Facebook, Twitter, Instagram and Snapchat can allow you to be more conversational and less formal; however, Linkedin has to be kept professional. The feedbacks of your customers will play a great role in building your brand image, so it is highly recommended to make good use of polls and giveaways to elicit consumer feedback. You can also make use of blogs or articles to provide detailed information about your business and company. This need not be mentioned that the content should be informative as well as interesting to retain the attention of the customers.

3. Establish your Brand Image

The biggest challenge one faces at the beginning of marketing campaigns on social media is to ensure that the company or the brand is noticed by the potential customers. The first step and the simplest technique is to ensure that your social media websites are well linked on your home page or any blog created by your company. The best part is that now the links are available in the form of buttons or logos created by the graphic designers. Every time you connect with your potential customers, you should be ready to talk about your social media pages in a catchy manner.

4. Give due Preference to Less Popular social media sites as well

In a lure to be visible on more popular social media sites, one shouldn't ignore the less talked about ones. Various start up and social media companies are emerging almost on a daily basis. You need to identify those which can cater to your company's vision and demographics. It's quite possible that such sites may not have a huge following like Facebook and Twitter, but they can certainly help in increasing your market share with potential new customers.

Highly effective tools are used by such sites which can make you more visible on the web. The best example is of Google+ which enhances the chances of getting good ranking on Google search engine mainly in local business section due to the availability of local business listings.

5. Keep Quality over Quantity.

Just focusing on quantity and keeping on posting any kind of content can never give one success in long run. One must avoid posting verbose content on social media as it may give a bad impression as well as a set back to your business marketing efforts. Apart from understanding what to post, you must also know when to post as posting at the peak time always gets more viewers. The social media is already flooded with content. In such a situation, the customers want to see relevant content as its said quality always wins over quantity.

To understand this on a deeper level, think about one of your connections on Facebook who keeps posting irrelevant content every few hours. So, you must give importance only to such content which can be duly appreciated by others and create such an impression that people keep waiting for you to post new content. So, always think twice before posting any kind of information on social media platforms.

6. Use Business Listing Report.

To gain maximum benefit and keep one's business tactics updated, a large number of small size and mid-size businesses make use of online directories. You must have an organized market plan to boost your marketing strategies. By implementing online directories, you can accumulate immense benefits from your marketing and advertising strategy. This is also recommended as you get a lot of customer attention at a very low investment. Online directories can play a significant role in boosting your business by increasing the website traffic and making your market presence felt by finding prospective customers. It certainly improves bottom line revenue of your business to a large extent. Online directories in combination with social media strategies can prove to be a powerful potion for your business.

7. Act Now without Delay

It is important for every entrepreneur to understand the fact that the time to embrace social media is always as soon as possible as it gets updated very frequently. As you delay, your chances to be left behind in the social media marketing forum increases. Don't be scared of taking the first step, but be confident of reaching new heights by following the social media marketing tips. The fact can't be denied that social media is a platform where one can meet a maximum number of potential customers in a short span of time. In fact, you need to be present everywhere as customers can search for your products and services on any of the platforms. It's undoubtedly true that social media is going to stay and keep playing a pivotal role in marketing for one's business or brand image.

So, the best suggestion will be to embrace it as soon as possible and also start implementing the latest apps and techniques to enjoy the growth of your business and brand. Use that chance, don't stay behind, get in front of everyone else and show them the way to go. Be someone they will look up to. Social media gives you the opportunity to do exactly that, and they are trying even harder to help you with their platforms created especially for your brand.

CONCLUSION

As a business leader, you have the responsibility of upholding your business' brand to the highest standards. You have to be strategic and creative when adopting new tactics to grow your audience. Social media is a golden opportunity that is almost a given in today's digital society. Thank you for choosing to read this guide. Before you go off to begin building your audience and posting to social media, remember to begin with your goal in mind. Let's quickly recap goals and ways to engage on each platform.

- As a Facebook user, you engage your target audience in order to increase traffic to the website and generate leads. You engage on Facebook by asking questions to open up discussions, sharing photos, sharing relevant articles and connecting with stakeholders.

- On Twitter, you interact with your target audience in order to acquire new customers. You can engage your followers by leveraging hashtags, resharing content of collaborators and sharing interesting photos and relevant articles.

- Instagram is where you can promote and share company culture to help generate leads. You engage consumers by sharing interesting and visually appealing content.

- Snapchat is where you tell your business' story in order to engage better with consumers. You can tell the story with behind-the-scenes content, events and mobile-only offers.

- LinkedIn is good if you decide to look for employers for yourself or employees for your brand. You update your resume, you look for experience and exist as a professional in the virtual world.

- Pinterest is the place where you save or share pins you like. The place to offer your brand particularly if it attracts customers through visual stimulation, like home design items or clothes.

- Flickr is the social network for photographers, both professional and amateur. They can engage and learn, present their skills and talents to the world, and possibly get noticed or hired.

You want to understand how your brand is growing and who you are reaching on each social network you're investing time. By studying the results of your efforts, you can see what's working and what isn't and modify behaviors based on what you find. While this guide provides you with some metrics to monitor, there are other websites and guides available that will provide you with even more information for gathering and understanding social media analytics.

Educate yourself continually on everything you do, be the one who is thirsty for knowledge, be the one who is innovative and groundbreaking, be the brand for yourself. Achieve that through smart work, not hard work. You have so many possibilities and options at hand. Find your target audience, reach your goals, be better with every single day, don't neglect what you have created and certainly don't let it get out of control. Show your ideas to the world and change the world if you have to. This is an opportunity - you just have to seize it!

A very important part of raising brand awareness through social media channels is certainly interaction with the customers. Whether you own a small upcoming brand or a huge brand that is already well known, interaction with the customers will only make your brand seem even more serious and customer oriented.

What is more, people today seem to love hype and some pretty crazy stuff so it is no longer enough to create content that is just relevant. The big brands are using hype content to make their social posts relevant and viral, and you should be doing the same. While many of us may not love hype, it is what sells today, and when it comes to marketing, we need to give the customers what they want, not what we think is best.

We are in a digital age. The prominence of social media branding will continue to grow and become increasingly important in the coming years. You have already taken steps to be ahead of the curve and put your business on a path to branding success!

Free Bonus: Join Our Book Club and Receive Free Gifts Instantly

Free Bonus "<u>Instant Access</u>" Click Below For Your **Bonus**: https://goo.gl/UgTgnW